RGP
RIO GRANATA PRESS

RGP

RIO GRANATA PRESS

THE STORY
OF THE STORY

WHAT I WROTE AND WHY

NORMA LIBMAN

Published in USA
ISBN 978-0-9914775-2-4

Also by Norma Libman
Historical Fiction
Lonely River Village

For Children
Hannah's Day at School

www.NormaLibman.com

RIO GRANATA PRESS

Cover illustration and book design:
Gary W. Priester
Author photo: Mary E. Carter

FOR

David, Lorie, Chuck, Shari, Rochelle, Rhoda.
And in memory of Alan, and my parents,
Ruth and Morris.

INTRODUCTION

I WASN'T SUPPOSED to be a writer.

And yet.

I grew up in a home in Chicago that was filled with books. Bookcases lined the walls of our living room and dining room and bedrooms. At one point my parents bought three or four new bookcases and put them down the middle of the living room and called it a room divider. They were quite pleased with their dual-purpose wall and didn't mind that one already small room was now two even smaller rooms. Later they built an addition to the house, a room that was to serve as an office for my father, and shifted the bookcase room dividers into the new room and we had our old living room back.

Books were revered. Reading was encouraged and lauded. No subject was off-limits. We could read anything, though my father did frown on comic books. Still, he didn't forbid them, just let us know we could do better. And I did read everything I could get my hands on. During summers I would ride my bike to the library every two weeks. The bicycle had a basket in front of the handlebars that would comfortably hold fourteen books, all from the juvenile section. That was the limit a child could borrow, and the maximum time allowed for keeping the books was two weeks. It worked out perfectly; I read a book a day, all summer long. This was when I was approximately between the ages of eight and twelve, in the early 1950's. I never attended summer camp – it was never even discussed as an option as my parents likely could not have afforded it in those days – so I had plenty of time. And of course I was one of those kids who read with a flashlight under the covers in bed at night, so that opened up another whole block of reading time for me.

But who were the writers of all these books in my house – mostly histories, especially about World War II and the Holocaust, and all the current novels as they appeared on the best-seller lists – that my parents kept purchasing and trying to "find room for"? They certainly weren't people we knew personally. With one exception. My mother sort of knew Saul Bellow and he was one of the most important writers of the day, a winner of the Nobel Prize in Literature, no less. She had gone to school with him. They were two years apart and weren't friends but she knew who he was. He was weird, she said. I never knew exactly what she meant by that and it was hardly a professional opinion. But did she, and maybe my father as well, form their view of writers based on that slim thread of experience? The general feeling was that writing was not a "normal" profession. It was not what "regular" people did to earn a living. Of my brother Alan, who was to become the editor of a professional journal, my parents said he was "doing his own thing" when asked what his occupation was. I think they just didn't have the vocabulary to describe a career that was even remotely literary. They saw themselves as regular, middle-class people, striving to raise normal children.

So there was a love of books. And, ironically, a sort of disdain for the people who wrote them. Despite this mixed message, I wrote my first "book" at age eight. Probably more like a longish short story, it was a mystery in the style of Nancy Drew, the girl detective that all my friends and I were reading. (The boys, of course, were reading The Hardy Boys series.) That was all I knew of mysteries at the time and I invented a teenage girl protagonist – I can no longer remember her name – who solved a problem I also can't remember. I drew a map of the town to help me plot the story. As best as I recall, if a stranger had picked up the manuscript and read it she would have judged it to have been written by an eight-year-old. I was no prodigy. But I wanted to be a writer, even though I didn't think it was an actual job someone could aspire to or study for.

Writing as a profession remained outside the norm for our family. I was told I could be a teacher, and I did become one. More on that later. And, no, it is not lost on me: the irony of the name they gave me, Norma, these parents who wanted us to be just like everyone else, to be *normal*.

I complained about my name once.

"Why didn't you name me Susie or Judy or Linda? Like other people? Regular names?" I asked them.

"You were named for Norma Talmadge," my mother said.

She was a famous film actress I had never heard of – her heyday was well before my time, in the era of silent films.

"And you should be happy with that name," she said, "we had been considering Minnie."

As it turns out that really would have been a disaster since I'm short. After the mini-skirt came into fashion in the sixties, and mini took on the meaning of small, the jokes would never have stopped.

I became a writer more or less by accident. It was something I could do to earn extra money after I abandoned teaching elementary school in favor of staying home with my three children. I started writing for textbook publishers, moved on to newsletters for non-profits, public relations materials, and finally newspaper writing, which introduced me to meatier material. I wrote a few short stories here and there, mostly for fun, but never got any of them published. It was newspaper writing that finally captured my interest. It's worth noting, by the way, that in my generation and my children's there are now several writers in the family. And I see quite a bit of literary promise among my grandchildren. Maybe there was a genetic tendency for writing all along and it could not be crushed.

In the end, I wrote more than five hundred articles, published in newspapers nationwide, most of them for the *Chicago Tribune*, some of which they syndicated. I wrote as a freelancer while resuming a teaching career as an adjunct instructor of English and Humanities at a community college. When I was in my fifties I expanded my focus to include, in addition to the general run of newspaper feature articles, three new areas of research: writers of the secret Chinese script, Nu Shu; nineteenth-century American women pioneers; and Crypto-Jews, descendants of Jews expelled from Spain during fifteenth century Inquisitional times who continued to practice their religion in secret – some even until the present. I used what I was learning about these subjects to write the occasional article. I also wrote lectures that I delivered to adult audiences in continuing education venues, and as a lecturer and tour guide for programs in New Mexico, where I moved from Chicago in 1996. Some of the Nu Shu material became part of my first book.

But the most important development that came out of that move and shift in focus was a reevaluation of my writing, of myself, of my life. And it happened because the stories I became so absorbed in were about people, women primarily, who preserved something of themselves and something of their culture because they either wrote, or told, or sometimes both, the stories of their lives.

Finally, it was Shi-lin, a young Chinese woman somewhere in the Hunan Province of China, sometime prior to the Communist Revolution, who woke me up to this deeper work. I encountered her story, embroidered in Nu Shu – a secret writing system invented by pre-Communist Chinese women, woven into table cloths, fans, and other household linens. It was this woman who first got me thinking about secret stories. She sewed the characters in order to hide the fact she was writing, and in order to dull the pain of the beatings from her mother-in-law. In order to forget that she could only see her baby son for one hour a day because her mother-in-law did not think Shi-lin was fit to raise him. This was just part of the story she told in her sewing.

After I wrote an article about Nu Shu for the *Chicago Tribune*, people contacted me with information about other secrets revealed by women in the stories they told. This is when I first heard about the Crypto-Jews. How they passed down the secret of their true religion from generation to generation. How they remembered the rituals without books or rabbis to instruct them. This brought men into the fabric of storytelling. I wanted to know about them, too.

People told me about the women who pioneered their way across the western part of the American continent, the earliest of them venturing into territory which was not yet officially part of the United States. Who ran the show behind the scenes, cooking and mending and treating the sick, making it possible for the whole operation to proceed in a fairly civilized manner. What stories must they have had, I wondered. And when I found the stories I wasn't disappointed.

These three sets of stories and all the others from the hundreds of people I interviewed for newspaper articles were right there in front of me, but I didn't know they were connected. They wouldn't settle down. They wouldn't march in an orderly fashion. They wouldn't sort themselves into a neat row and announce their meaning, explain to me what I was supposed to learn from them. When I moved to New Mexico and was doing less newspaper writing, I thought that was the time to arrange it all into a book and make some sense of them. But they still wouldn't cooperate.

Then I knew other stories were in the way. My own stories, my own history. Maybe not in the way. Maybe just dancing around the circle and weaving in and out and calling attention to themselves when I was trying to think of other people's lives. Always it has been my practice to write down ideas as they come to me, even during the night if necessary, not only so I won't forget them, but also so I can get them out of my mind and stop the endless circular thinking they can cause. I began to listen for my own stories and write about myself, in little bits and pieces at first, and then with more ease, and finally in great torrents.

Amazingly, writing about myself freed me to write more easily about the new material I was finding. Something resembling chapters of a book – a book about me and lots of other people, too – began to pile up. Not in any recognizable order, of course. That would be too easy. No, this was just notes from research and interviews, all mixed up with original writings. You could hardly call it a book yet.

Still, in time, it did start to make some sense. I saw the thread that ran through it all. These people told their stories, either by talking or writing or even sewing them if that was what was necessary to preserve them. And they listened. They told the stories and people listened to them. They heard each other. *They* survived because their stories survived.

The book that came out of all this remembering and scribbling is the story of a writing life – mine – and the lives of some of the people I encountered during my career. Ghosts of people, especially the Nu Shu ladies, who told their stories long ago and whose lives I would like to think I helped rescue from oblivion; and people I interviewed, who shared with me bits of their lives that were important to them. Eventually I saw that I had learned something from the lives I had entered, though it wasn't always clear what. I did see that everyone's life is a story worth saving and telling and I'm happy to have had a part in doing that for a few people. And I'm now more able to see that my own story is also worth saving and telling.

So here goes: What I learned about these people. And what I learned about myself in the process. And, more important, what I continue to learn as I hear the stories and digest the memories. I am still listening to them. And I am listening to myself.

CHAPTER ONE

I AM A WRITER. More specifically, a journalist. My path to this career did not include journalism school, or even one course in writing, aside from the required rhetoric (do they still call it that?) of my college freshman curriculum. I was trained, instead, to be a teacher and I was one – everything from third grade to college at various times in my life. But when my three children were still quite little, I started writing feature stories for newspapers and magazines and for many years was a regular freelance writer for the *Chicago Tribune*. After a while I took to calling myself an independent journalist and I still think that title is an apt description.

By the mid-eighties I was writing regularly for several sections of the *Tribune* – the woman's section, the travel section, the Sunday magazine – and occasionally my byline might appear elsewhere in the paper as well. It was fun. I met – and wrote stories about – some of the most amazing people: advice columnist Ann Landers, violinist Itzhak Perlman, Amy Tan of *The Joy Luck Club* fame, author, radio host and local Chicago celebrity Studs Terkel, Madam Jehan Sadat, wife of Egyptian President Anwar Sadat, TV host and newsman Charles Kuralt, Donald Rumsfeld of the Bush era, O.J. Simpson six months before, well, you know, and hundreds of others. Little guys as well as big guys. Good guys and bad guys, though to be honest I wasn't aware that any of them would turn out to be bad guys at the time I met them.

This was all great preparation for three of the big stories I worked on in the nineties: Nu Shu, American women pioneers, and the Crypto-Jews – more about them later. I learned patience trying to get an interview for three months with actor Carrie Fisher, for instance, and then finally being given an hour on the phone with her while she rode her exercise bicycle and couldn't get her breath to speak in full sentences. Or matching wits with the humorist, Dave Barry, in a tiny interview room at the *Tribune* building, and discovering I had no wit at all compared to his quick mind. I learned when to keep my mouth shut. Or going out on a story with a temperamental photographer who wanted to control the interview and said, "There'll be no story if I don't get my pictures." I said, "There'll be no story if I don't get my story." I learned when to open my mouth.

Right after the story of the Nu Shu ladies dropped into my lap another story, which I initially thought was related, appeared on the horizon. Actually, several stories seemed to be related and many of them came my way because of an author in Denver, Jacqueline Tobin, who had seen my syndicated *Chicago Tribune* Nu Shu article in *The Denver Post*. She contacted me and suggested that Nu Shu was just one of many examples of women preserving culture and history while the men of their community went about their business. Tobin, herself, was working on the story of American slave quilts that carried hidden directions for the underground railroad. This later became her excellent book, *Hidden in Plain View*.

Tobin thought we could find more examples of this phenomenon – secret stories that existed in a sort of underground culture –and do a book together. One of the stories that turned up at this time was the story of the Crypto-Jews. This was a community of descendants of the Spanish Inquisition who moved from Spain all over the world, including large numbers to the American Southwest, and continued to practice their Judaism in secret while professing to be Christians. Amazingly, there are still remnants of this community living this double life today. On my own, I began to find diaries written by American women pioneers, but put that on the back burner for a while.

Well, a writer has to make a decision. You simply cannot do everything, not at once anyway. But I couldn't decide between the Nu Shu story and the Crypto-Jewish story. Tobin eventually struck out on her own, having made her decision, and worked on the slave quilts. I kept working on those two that had the strongest pull on me, doing research, doing interviews, getting more and more swamped with material and more confused. Both stories had a place in my heart. Eventually, I decided there were significant differences between the two. The Crypto-Jewish women were, indeed, keeping a secret. But not from their men, who were in on the whole thing. Only the Nu Shu ladies stood alone against the world, even against their own husbands, and persevered. I felt a greater pull in their direction and decided to pursue that topic first.

CHAPTER TWO

My life of telling stories and being interested in other people's stories began very early. As a child I felt a strong responsibility for the education and entertainment of my younger brother, David. The two of us used to sit on the floor of the upstairs hall of our small home, long after we were supposed to be asleep at night. There were three bedrooms on the second floor of our house. One was for my parents, one for me, and one for the three boys in the family. Later, when I left for college, my much younger sister took over my room. The most intense period of making up stories probably occurred when I was around eight years old and David was five. Our baby brother, Alan, would have been asleep, and it was to be many years before our other siblings joined the family.

One of our favorite topics of conversation was the possibility that the two of us had been related in a previous life, but not as brother and sister. I remember explaining to David that maybe we had been George and Martha Washington. (See? I would say to him. Related, but not in the same way. He got it.) We imagined our lives in that previous incarnation and made up fabulous stories.

Or the past lives of our family, which we had to invent completely since we knew so little about what seemed to us a dark and secret history of life in "the old country," as our grandma always called it. We were put to bed quite early most every night in order to prevent us from falling prey to what my father considered waste-of-time television shows like *I Love Lucy*, and that gave us plenty of time to creep out of our bedrooms, meet in the hallway, and use our imaginations. (Our father did not like television, did not think it was "going anywhere," and thought most of what was on it was junk. As to the content of the programming he was right, of course, but we couldn't see that then. At the time we were just angry and our anger fueled our imaginations.)

During the daytime (on non-school days) when we didn't have to whisper, we had other games. In these we had the participation of our baby brother, Alan, who would eventually be the middle child of five. But at this time we were three and in our games this two-year-old played an adorable handful of a child we named Willem. I was Willem's mother and David played the unusual role of Uncle David. Nothing so mundane as Mommy and Daddy for us.

At the age of two Alan, the most even-tempered, good-natured baby who ever lived, could sit still on a sofa and pretend it was a train and no moving around was allowed. He could respond to the name Willem when the game was in progress and to Alan when we were in "real life." He never got bored of sitting still or tired of being carried around by his eight-year-old sister pretending to be his mother. He never cried or demanded anything. He never quit the game until David and I said it was over. If his diaper was wet he kept it to himself until his real mother came along to take over.

In one version of this game we were a city family. We sat on the sofa while I pretended to drive Uncle David and Willem wherever we needed to go. At other times we pretended to live on a farm (we had a rocking horse in the basement that was used for that one). In still another game we lived in the Wild West. At no time did we ever feel it necessary to invent a husband for me or a father for Willem. I have no idea what we were thinking of; this was still the early fifties and there were absolutely no examples of such an avant-garde family anywhere in our lives. Yet there it is. We played that game for as long as Alan remained small enough to carry around.

When two more siblings entered the picture and we all grew up, Alan became the glue that held our family together. Maybe it was because he was the middle child, bridging the gap between two older and two younger siblings that stretched over a span of almost fifteen years in age. Maybe it was because he had a special talent for remembering birthdays and organizing celebrations. Or maybe it was just because he always had time for everyone. One of his friends told me that she used to call him at work and sometimes she started talking and didn't know when to stop. "He'd never cut me off or tell me he was busy," she said. "Sometimes I'd hear the computer keys start to click and I'd know I'd gone on too long." Another friend of his told me, "He never had an enemy. I would have liked to give him some of mine."

The last time I saw Alan was Father's Day, 1989. He was walking backwards down the sidewalk of my house, waving and saying goodbye after our family get-together. Come on, Alan, I thought. Turn around. You'll trip. At last he did turn but I can't remember how he looked walking away. I must have gone into the house and turned my attention to other matters.

The whole family had been at my house celebrating Father's Day: my parents, siblings, husband, children, niece and nephew. Alan had arrived first for the gathering and brought me a book. It was the new Anne Tyler novel, hot off the press, and he'd already finished reading it. Stories, still, but Alan was more of a reader than a teller or imaginer of stories. He always kept up with the latest fiction and let me read whatever I wanted when he was finished. Usually I picked something from his bookcases. This must be a good one, I thought; he didn't usually make the selection for me.

When Alan left our house he probably lit a cigarette before he started his car. Alan never smoked in front of the family. He believed that *we* believed he had kicked a three pack-a-day habit. We could always detect the smell of smoke on him, though, and knew from his friends that he still smoked.

Some months before, he and I had traveled to Los Angeles to visit a cousin who was terminally ill and who died the day after we arrived. Under the stress of the visit and funeral Alan smoked and asked me not to tell our parents. That's how he was. At 39 he wasn't afraid to be caught smoking by his mother and father. He just didn't want them to worry and he knew they worried plenty about this single vice: smoking. He had a congenital heart defect which had caused a heart attack 14 years earlier when he was only 25 and he was fighting a very high cholesterol level. The doctor who put him on a cholesterol-reducing diet told him that if he couldn't manage to adhere to the diet while giving up cigarettes, he should just quit smoking and forget the diet. He did the diet and kept on smoking.

Still, Alan was the picture of good health: almost six feet tall, blond hair just beginning to thin and recede, blue eyes, slim build, even before the diet, an infectious smile and a bubbling personality. His placid disposition as a young child had developed into a very sweet nature. He had what seemed like a million friends and they would all attest to the fact that Alan was the most loyal, generous and helpful person they had ever known.

Alan did things for people, the sort of things you don't notice until suddenly no one is doing them anymore. He was our family's calendar and conscience. There'd be the phone call: It's almost time for David's birthday. Shall we go in on something together? Let's do something different – this is a big one. Without much trouble on anyone's part the plans fell into place.

On the Wednesday following Father's Day Alan had dinner out with some friends. He returned home sometime before 9:00 and phoned our sister in Washington. She wasn't home and he left a message. Then he phoned his former wife, who lived in New York. The two of them had remained close during the seven or eight years since their divorce. She, too, was not at home so again he left a message.

Then Alan went to bed. During the night his heart broke and by morning he was gone.

CHAPTER THREE

IT'S NOT SURPRISING that I gravitated toward feature writing at newspapers. I was always interested in language and human interest stories. I loved interviewing authors, hoping to learn something about how they did what they did. But I never tried to write a book (unless you count my childhood attempt at that mystery) until after I had been writing short newspaper pieces for at least twenty years.

My interest in language took me to the brink of considering an advanced degree in linguistics, but I gave that up for lack of time and, probably, determination. It started early in my life. By the age of six I was tormenting my mother with questions about spelling. "What is 'way-ter,' I asked her one day when I returned from school. I had passed a manhole cover with the work 'water' embossed on it and I explained that was where I saw the strange word. "It's 'water,' she said. "It can't be," I answered. "That would need two t's."

Around the same time I asked her what an "onion" prayer book was. I was looking at the books in one of our bookcases. She informed me the it was 'union' not 'onion.' "'Un' is pronounced 'un' I informed her. 'Onion' should be spelled 'union.' I had the same complaint about 'divide' when I spelled it 'devide' in a spelling bee at school and was called out. My mother, exasperated at times, could only say, "Well that's how the English language is. Don't ask me why." I suppose at some point I just accepted the system, such as it is, as we all do. I learned how to spell and just got on with it.

I'd been writing newspaper articles for about fifteen years when I first encountered the story of Nu Shu, a story that fit into my love of language and my interest in people's lives. How I found it was mostly by accident. I learned much of the story while at a writers' conference in Taipei, Taiwan in 1994, though it had started in the Hunan Province of China an unknown many years back in history. At the time, I knew nothing of the Nu Shu except what I'd heard from my editor at the *Chicago Tribune*. And he knew very little and wasn't impressed. Just something I might look into if I had time between meetings, he said. I didn't think it was much either until I heard about Shi-lin and some of the others. How they learned the Nu Shu, which simply means "women's writing," from their older sisters, mothers, grandmothers, or their girlfriends. How they kept the Nu Shu as a secret writing system with their friends. And finally, when they were married out by their families, how they kept the secret from their husbands.

It all happened somewhat in a rush. I'd interviewed and written a story for the *Chicago Tribune* about a woman, Ching Bezine, born in China and raised in Taiwan, who was an author of books in both Chinese and English. Some months after her story appeared in the paper Bezine called and asked me to join a small party of writers on a trip to Taipei to be part of an Asian writers' conference that was including Western writers for the first time.

I accepted on the spot. A free trip to Taiwan? Who wouldn't? The details unfolded and I learned that five writers from the United States were to be selected by Ching, who had attended this conference several times as an Asian writer. Ching's mission was to choose different types of writers and we were each to present to the conference a picture of life in the U.S. for writers in our field. I was chosen to represent freelance journalism. I started to work on my presentation at once and informed one of the editors I worked for frequently, at what was then the woman's section of the *Chicago Tribune*, that I was on my way to the Far East, all expenses paid, to talk about the writing life in the U.S.

He told me that he'd had a story on his desk for a year: Nu Shu, some kind of secret writing system of Chinese women, being translated by a women's organization in Taiwan. He didn't know much more. Not important enough, he said, to pay someone to go over there. But if I was going anyway, maybe I should take a look, he said.

"See what you can find out. Take photos if it warrants. Let me know when you get back. Don't worry if you don't have time. I don't know if I'd publish anything about it anyway." And so on.

Any time a freelancer can pick up a story on the way to something else she grabs it. Cost effective. Nothing to lose by trying. So I took the little bit of information he had and left with it. There was never any doubt that I would at least look into it. And I started my looking even before I left for the conference. I checked with the organization that had sent the information to my editor. I checked with Ching, who had never heard of Nu Shu. And I called a source in Taiwan and set up a meeting with one of the women who had worked on the translation of Nu Shu into Mandarin Chinese.

But, really, I didn't have much when I landed in Taipei. The story had fallen into my lap and I was excited about it, but at the same time I was overwhelmed by the different culture I was experiencing and nervous about the prospect of delivering my talk to an audience of Chinese-speaking writers who would actually hear my words from a translator. Though, in truth, most of them could understand English quite well and could have managed without a translator. This just added to my sense of inferiority since at that point I understood not one word of Chinese.

There was an underlying agenda to the meeting that I was not aware of until I arrived at the Grand Hotel – and it is grand! – in Taipei, and received the schedule for our week of activities. We were to be taken all over the city to visit not only tourist sites but the Ministry of Education and other government offices. We were to meet all manner of dignitaries right up to the Prime Minister. And we were to be fed the most elegant and expensive food at every meal. The agenda, it turned out, was to show off Taiwan in the best possible light so that we would return to the United States and not only write about our visit, but lobby on behalf of this struggling democracy for a place in the United Nations. Obviously they had an exaggerated notion of our power and status at home.

The effect of all this was that there was no free time for me to investigate Nu Shu. I literally had to ask permission to get one afternoon off to conduct an interview with the woman involved in the translating of Nu Shu into Mandarin. Permission was grudgingly given. The fear was that in seeing something that was not orchestrated by the government I might see something that was not favorable to Taiwan. What? Crime? Dirt? I never knew for sure, but I do know that when they took us to the Ministry of Education they would not let us go to the bathroom. They insisted there was simply no time. Later I learned that they were ashamed that the bathrooms in that building were the old-fashioned ones where you had to squat over a hole in the floor. They preferred to risk discomfort on the part of their guests rather than let us know the truth: that they were not quite as modern as they were pretending to be.

We had shark fin soup at every meal except breakfast, every day. At one point, about midway during the visit, I turned to the man sitting next to me at one of our lavish dinners and said, "Shark fin soup must be a very popular dish here."

"Oh, no, we never eat it," he answered.

"Then why have I had it at every meal?" I asked.

"We want you to have the best. But we never eat shark fin soup. Too rich, too expensive for the ordinary person."

So. I was not an "ordinary" person. I was special. I ate shark fin soup at every meal. It was put in front of me and I ate it, along with pig's ears and fish eyeballs and all the other delicacies that special people eat in the East. But all I really wanted to do was find out about the Nu Shu ladies. They were so tantalizingly close and yet so far.

Finally, on the fourth day of our meeting, I was given my freedom for one afternoon and I escaped to have lunch (no shark fin soup) with Su Chien-ling, who had organized the translation of the Nu Shu into Mandarin with the help of the Awakening Foundation, a women's activist group in Taiwan.

Su took me to a little neighborhood restaurant where I had the only "real" meal I was to experience in the Taipei part of the trip. I remember nothing of the food; for me it was all about what I was hearing from Su, who had been educated in the United States and was fluent in English. She told me of the Nu Shu ladies and the efforts of her organization to translate their writings into Mandarin. She told me how the writing was first found. (An elderly woman had written directions in Nu Shu to her childhood home and when she arrived in town it was so changed that she couldn't find the house. She took the directions to the police station and when they couldn't read the Nu Shu they called in a professor to help them figure out what the writing was.) She told me why it was being translated in Taiwan and not in China. (They couldn't find anyone interested enough to do it on the mainland.) She told me that some of it was written but much of it was embroidered into textiles, making it both art and literature at the same time, not to mention history. And she told me a few of the stories, which included diary entries about day-to-day life, heartbreaking stories of family tragedies, letters to friends and relatives, even retelling of old folk tales.

I listened. That is a skill you learn as an interviewer. The interview is not a social conversation. Or it is a very lopsided one. The interviewee should be doing most of the talking. The interviewer asks a question and then keeps quiet until the question is answered, or close to it.

The Awakening Foundation had published a book of Nu Shu writings translated into Mandarin. There were one thousand copies of the book in print and she gave me one.

I was hooked. Completely. I wanted to know these women and their stories. And, more, I wanted other people to know them, too. Unfortunately, there was a big barrier between me and these women. Ironically, it was language, exactly what the Nu Shu story was about. In all innocence, I believed I could knock down that barrier easily, in one of two ways. Either I would get someone to convert all the translated stories from Mandarin into English for me, or I would learn Chinese and do it myself. Ladies and gentleman, I was not a twenty-year-old kid at the time. I was a seasoned woman in her fifties. With her head in the sand, apparently. I can barely believe now, some two dozen years later, that I was so naïve at the time. On the other hand, had I been more realistic I would have bid the Nu Shu ladies adieu on the island of Taiwan and moved on to other things. Had that happened I would have missed out on knowing some of the most brilliant, inventive, beautiful, resilient women who ever lived. Perhaps it was the example of the Nu Shu ladies themselves, who never gave up, that prevented me from giving up on them and their story.

But just for laughs, let me tell you about my attempt to learn Mandarin.

I was living in New Mexico by this time and I got myself into a Continuing Education program from the University of New Mexico. There were about a dozen people in the class and, except for myself and one man, all the rest were preparing for their trip to China to adopt a baby girl – this was all the rage at that time. The man was Chinese, spoke Cantonese, and needed Mandarin for business reasons. I remarked that this must be easy for him. "Not at all," he said. "I can't understand a word of Mandarin." That should have been my first clue.

As probably many people know, every word in Mandarin has four tonal qualities, and each carries a different meaning. You must master these subtle differences if you are to speak and understand the language. My poor hearing alone disqualified me, not to mention my inability to carry a tune. The teacher would say a word and then walk around the room listening to each person repeat the word individually. "Good, good, excellent," she'd remark as she made her happy way around the classroom. Then she would get to me. "Ooooh," she'd say through gritted teeth. I gave up.

That left my Mandarin translations of Nu Shu in the hands of four wonderful people who would translate the Mandarin into English for me. I'm not sorry it turned out that way. They did an excellent job and gave me insights into Chinese culture I never would have had if it hadn't been for them. But still, it was to be several more years before I would find a way to tell these stories that did honor to the women who wrote them.

CHAPTER FOUR

"THEY TOOK THE FIRE POKER and beat me with it until my head was bleeding. My mother-in-law said, 'Don't kill her because if she dies it will cost more money to get another wife.' One day I was so hungry I stole a turnip that was meant to feed the pig and they beat me again. Some days they starve me and won't let me have even one sip of tea but still I have to do my work. Once they dumped me in the latrine because I was so hungry I couldn't work very hard."

Yes, this really happened. To an unknown woman who lived in a small village in the Hunan Province of China. When? We are not sure, but it was before the Communist Revolution, since after that event, when women were allowed to attend school, there would be no need for a woman to write her story in the form that this one was written: a secret writing system called Nu Shu. It is a system invented by women so they could communicate with each other in writing even though none of them had been to school or learned to write Mandarin. And because they did not want it known by their husbands that they could communicate in this way, they embroidered most of it, on table cloths, fans, napkins, handkerchiefs, even the cloth used for binding the feet of little girls.

What incredible spirit, I thought when I first encountered these stories. I'd spent some time reading diaries of American women pioneers of the nineteenth century and was always amazed that those women had the energy to write at the end of a day which included walking many miles, caring for children, preparing meals in the outdoors, and braving all sorts of weather. They did this, and more, for months on end. Here, now, in the Nu Shu, I was reading the words of women who had endured even harder lives, often suffered beatings, and yet managed to learn a writing system in secret in order to preserve their thoughts and experiences, and communicate them to others. Besides, many of these women would live their entire lives this way, some for a few years until the birth of a son accorded them a bit more status in the family. Few had any hope for relief in the short run. (I've written and lectured about the hardships both these sets of women have endured. My audiences have included males and females. Many men have questioned that these terrible things could have actually happened. No woman has ever raised an objection. I'll leave it at that.)

The method for learning this writing system was primitive, and at the same time so intimate as to provide much more to learner and teacher than mere education. An older sister, mother, grandmother, aunt, friend, or female cousin would put her hand over the young girl's hand and guide her through the formation of the various characters. (Unlike Mandarin, which has some 50,000 characters, Nu Shu has about 1,500 and a girl could learn to communicate with as few as 300 characters.) In a small group of her own peers, guided by an older woman, the girl would learn to embroider the symbols she was learning to write. Like a sewing circle or other small gathering of women working together, these occasions allowed the girls to form close bonds with each other, bonds that would last a lifetime, even though the girls were doomed to be separated by the time they reached their mid-teens.

The girls were separated, even in their early teens, because of marriage. Each would, in due time, be "married out" to a family, likely in another village, in an arrangement that was strictly financial. The strong emotional bonds of these girls' lives were with their girlfriends, not with their husbands, whom they did not even know prior to going to live with them. The Nu Shu allowed them to continue their close relationships with their friends. They could pour their hearts out in the embroidery of a table cloth and napkins and then send the linens as a gift to their friend – often carried back to their old village by the unknowing husband, on a business trip, perhaps – and let the friend know how life was treating them.

I loved the Nu Shu ladies from the start. I'm a journalist, but also wear the writing teacher hat and have often heard the excuse from students that they are too tired or too busy to write. Here were women who worked from sun-up to sun-down for no money and probably little satisfaction. They were sometimes physically abused. They had been taken away from their birth families and often from the village in which they grew up. They were physically separated from their close friends. But because they *could* write (and sew!) at the end of the long, hard day, they had a built-in support system that saved many of their lives. In fact, some researchers have found that the suicide rate for women in this part of China was generally lower than elsewhere in that country during the pre-Communist twentieth century. I don't know if there are any studies going further back in time, and we don't know exactly where Nu Shu was invented or how old it is.

With no psychologists or psychiatrists to guide them, these women found comfort in their old friends, whom they kept near to their hearts for life. Their ability to write the language they had taught themselves made this possible. Even when the husbands were aware that their wives were creating more than mere decoration, they were not particularly interested in the details of "women's work" and left them alone as long as they did their required chores. Oddly, mothers-in-law, too, if they grew up in the same province, knew what their daughters-in-law were doing when they embroidered their table cloths, but they left them alone. Perhaps this is part of the same phenomenon that allowed mothers to bind the feet of their daughters despite the pain that ritual had caused the mothers. It was part of the culture and, for the most part, not questioned.

And it should be no surprise that this is not the only culture where women were compromised, took their fates into their own hands, and found some way to save their sanity. Historically, it has happened in many times and places, not necessarily without the knowledge of men. There were private women's languages and messages sent by way of tied knots in scarves in parts of Africa. There were "painted prayers" on the sides of homes in India. Slaves sewed directions to the underground railroad into quilts in the American South. But these writers of Nu Shu did something else besides save themselves. They also provided a look at family life in rural China prior to the Communist Revolution as seen through the eyes of the women. Most everything else we have from that period comes from the pens of male historians.

No wonder I fell in love with the Nu Shu ladies: spunk, brains, perseverance. What a story. But at first that story was largely hidden from historians because people not acquainted with this culture simply saw the embroidery as decoration. Su told me a little about some of the writings and gave me that copy of the translations her organization, the Awakening Foundation, had done of the Nu Shu. But as the translations were in Mandarin, I still had nothing. So I returned to the United States with enough material for an article in the *Chicago Tribune*, which I wrote and which ran in May, 1994, and not much else except a hunger to know more. That was the real beginning of the journey to find the Nu Shu ladies. And I feel that I did find them. In part because of my attempts to learn Chinese, as I've described, and also because of the people I met while tracking down the translations of the Mandarin, once I acknowledged that I couldn't do it myself. Both experiences taught me as much about Chinese culture – and in a deep way – as I learned in all the extensive reading I did. I feel that it's all a part of listening. I know I say this often, but it's so important: we must listen to everyone, including ourselves, in order to get the story.

CHAPTER FIVE

I HAD SO MANY QUESTIONS. Who invented the Nu Shu? How did it actually work? Why had it stayed in the southern area of China, rather than spreading all over that vast country? Why was it being translated in Taiwan and not China? How was the secret discovered?

But what most mystified me at first was the foot binding. I couldn't understand how anyone could do it, why anyone would do it, or how it was connected to Nu Shu. But I heard from Su, right in the beginning, that one of the places they found Nu Shu was on the cloths used to bind little girls' feet. It seems that mothers would embroider Nu Shu messages on the strips of cloth that would later be used to break the feet of their little girls, usually around the age of six, so that the feet would develop into the delicate lotus shape that men coveted. Although the mother had endured the pain of the process, she believed that if her daughter did not have those tiny feet the family would not be able to make a good marriage for her. And a good marriage was essential or the girl would continue to be a drain on the family she was born into. So the mother forced her daughter to suffer the same pain she had endured as a child

I learned that foot binding was not practiced everywhere in China, and not at all times in their history. It was practiced primarily in prosperous locales where women were not needed to work in the fields, as they could not have done that type of work on feet measuring three to five inches. The Hunan Province, and specifically the Jiangyong County, where Nu Shu thrived, was such a place. It was a fertile valley, almost completely surrounded by mountains. Life was good there, men worked the rich fields, and, for the most part, women stayed home and tended to domestic chores.

The physical landscape of the place also explains why Nu Shu did not travel elsewhere. The mountains provided a natural barrier, and prior to the mid-twentieth century travel beyond the mountains was extremely difficult. People traveled from village to village, but mostly stayed within their own county. So even though women often left their home village for marriage, they were not really that far from home. But on tiny broken feet women could not travel home for a visit without assistance. No telephones, no schooling, no way to communicate.

Sometimes they did return for visits, though, with their husbands or their grown sons to help them travel. Also, it was the custom for the girl to return home three days after the marriage and stay until it was almost time to deliver her first baby. (Marriage dates were calculated so the young wife could become pregnant immediately and a three-day leeway was given.)

After the birth of a child the wife usually remained with her new husband's family except for unusual circumstances. But the Nu Shu could travel for her. And did, often in the arms of her oblivious husband or some other man from the village. It might be a table-cloth or a fan or a handkerchief. And it arrived at its destination as a gift meant for personal or domestic use. But it carried, in the beautiful needlework designs, information from its sender.

The story of the foot binding, which kept the women virtual prisoners in their husband's family's homes just drained me. Even the simple way I pictured it – before I knew the details – was horrible. But the real process, when I learned it, was far worse than anything I had ever imagined.

It's not just that the feet of the little girls, around six years old, were wrapped up so they couldn't grow large. It was far more sinister than that. The toes were bent back and sewed to the soles of the feet. The girls were made to walk back and forth continuously so the bones would break and so they would learn to take little, mincing steps, in the provocative manner of the tiny-footed beauties of their culture. The bandages were changed regularly and the wounds were cleaned so they wouldn't become infected. A good mother was required to know the correct way to do this.

Surely the mothers, who had suffered the same fate as children, must have cried to see their little daughters in pain. Personal accounts I have read tell how the girls shed tears for months as they got used to walking on crippled feet.

The finished product was not just a tiny foot, three to five inches in length and the smaller the better. It was a foot that, when turned over, had the exquisite shape of the lotus flower. The more perfect the shape and the tinier the foot the more prized the girl would be as a marriage prospect. Simply put, the prettier the foot the more a young man's family would have to pay, in money or gifts to the girl's parents, so the richer the husband would be. In exchange for a lifetime of pain and incapacitation – and I think we all know how miserable even a sore toe can make us feel – a young girl could be assured of having a life of financial comfort, if not of happiness.

But like it or not, foot binding is part of this story. If this had not been a prosperous area of China, the women may not have had the time to develop Nu Shu. Unfortunately, along with prosperity came foot binding. Still, not all girls suffered the procedure. The few who did not, worked harder in a physical sense because they were able to help with plowing the fields or gathering wood for fires or selling flowers at the market. Not to mention all the household duties they could perform. But they had made bad marriages, financially speaking, and didn't have maids to do this work for them. And the truth is some women did work at heavy labor, even with bound feet, because of changing fortunes in the family or just because her in-laws were mean or angry people. In most of Chinese history it was a lose-lose situation for women.

Well, in much of the history of the world it's been a tough go for women. In under-developed areas their lives might be spent almost exclusively in transporting water for the family. Even in more advanced countries, the right to vote is relatively newly won and many career paths are still off-limits for women. I knew that, but I hadn't encountered it with such immediacy until I read the stories of the Nu Shu ladies. And that's exactly why I couldn't give up on them. It's as though they were asking me to get their stories out. To do one little thing for them, nothing much in light of what they had accomplished by writing the stories in secret and at great risk to themselves.

I stuck with it. After trying – and failing, as I've already mentioned – to learn Chinese myself, I found four people to translate into English the stories that had been put into Mandarin by the Awakening Foundation. What much later became a failed attempt at a non-fiction book on the subject, a failed attempt at writing a collection of short stories, and finally, a successful novel based on the women's writings, started with the fine work of these translators. I learned from them not only some of the women's stories, and much about Chinese culture, but also something about myself. It was a surprise to learn that although the details of our lives could not have been more different, these women and I had a lot in common. And, I believe, they have a lot in common with all peoples of the world, men and women alike, who just want their stories told and recognized. I had to pursue the project.

I'm pleased to say the novel I finally wrote, *Lonely River Village*, won several awards. I believe the awards came because the story struck a note with so many people. And I think this is very much the right time to tell it. It speaks to women's issues ranging from physical and mental abuse to limited access to education. These are men's issues, too, because men and women live together in every culture, and impact each other. When women suffer, men's lives are diminished as well. I was able to include men in the story as a number of women described their fathers, brothers, and husbands, good and bad.

CHAPTER SIX

THE STORIES WOVE IN AND OUT of my mind, of my life. I continued to write for the paper. I followed research on the Nu Shu writing system that seemed to grow daily on the Internet. I began to find books on the subject, including one by a man who received his PhD studying and analyzing the writing. And the story of the Crypto-Jews was still there, nagging at me. Men and women kept the secret together, but the women were the most haunting, silent as they were about their role in preserving their religion in secret. You had to know somebody who knew the stories or you'd never hear anything. It was an oral tradition. They passed it down to their daughters most of the time: how to prepare the food, when to fast, when to change the linens and wash their hands, how to light the candles on Friday night. It was the women who kept track of the details, especially concerning food and cleanliness.

There is so much to know; Judaism is a complicated religion, made more so if one has to practice it in secret. Without books, without rabbis, how were they to remember it all? But they had their ways. They remembered dates and rituals in songs and games, for example. Spain's Edict of Expulsion of 1492, which set the date for expulsion or conversion in March, and then extended it to August 2, 1492, a date fraught with mysterious implications, proved, ironically, to be a help to Jews going underground. It listed "Jewish behaviors" so servants and neighbors and anyone else interested could stay on the alert and turn someone in to the Office of the Inquisition if they observed them behaving as Jews after they claimed to have converted. Some Jews got possession of copies of the edict and took it with them if they fled Spain or just consulted it if they remained in Spain. Basically, it reminded them how to be Jewish.

It told observers to notice if the woman of the house frequently had headaches on Saturday and was unable to work. That would suggest she was pretending to be ill in order to rest on Saturday without it appearing that she was observing the Sabbath on that day instead of Sunday. Does she prepare meals on Friday afternoon that can be warmed over or eaten cold on Saturday so she doesn't have to cook on that day? Does she cook with olive oil instead of lard so she won't have to serve pork in any form to her family? Does she change the bed linens and table linens every Friday afternoon in preparation for the Sabbath? Does the family wash their hands before meals and before praying? Do they step outside the house on Saturday at dusk and look to the sky to see if three stars are present so they know the Sabbath is over?

The list goes on. I told you it is a complicated religion. There's no way it could have survived in secret among descendants of the forced converts if they hadn't had some help. Actually, many of the traditions and stories got mixed up over time anyway. In Belmonte, Portugal, for instance, descendants of the secret Jews who left

Spain and settled in Portugal speak of a St. Moses, whose birthday they celebrate when the Christians are celebrating Christmas. On the other hand, they know how to make their own matzo at Passover. How many open Jews can do that?

A word about the mysterious date of August 2, 1492: it's also the date Columbus sailed, and there have always been rumors he might have been a Jew, or a descendant of forced converts, who was looking for a safe place for Jews to settle if they chose to flee Spain. I doubt we'll ever know for sure since there's so little we really know about the origins of this man, but it's certainly possible. He knew Hebrew and kept at least one journal in Hebrew (though to be fair, any gentleman with a complete education at that time learned Latin, Greek, and Hebrew, and he had a gentleman's education). Many of his friends, including the closest advisors to Ferdinand and Isabella, were Conversos (the Spanish word for "convert," applied to any Jew who converted to Christianity, or the descendant of such a person). It was known that there were Jews in India and he brought with him on his first trip to the New World – which he thought was India when he landed – a translator who spoke Hebrew. Might he have been expecting to find Hebrew-speaking Jews? Another goal of his journey was to Christianize any so-called pagans he found, yet there were no priests among the 120 men he brought with him. Also, he dated his letters to his son not from the birth of Christ, but from the fall of the Second Temple, the Jewish way of counting the days at that time. The Jewish holiday that commemorates that act of destruction of the Temple, in the year 70,

Tisha B'Av, happens to fall around the second of August, but who's counting?

None of this proves anything about Columbus' religious background, but taken together it is suggestive of a possible Jewish connection, likely several generations back, if one exists at all.

Anyway, the Crypto-Jewish ladies were calling to me, too. They were saying: you don't know how we suffered, how we suffer still. They were different from the Nu Shu ladies in that respect. Many were still alive, were still living this dual life and suffering the consequences of having a double identity. Of going to Mass on Sunday and celebrating the start of the Sabbath on Friday night with a small group of friends in a secret house with a secret room that opened only onto a courtyard and not to the street. Of having to teach their daughters how to be Jewish and at the same time to keep the secret of their Judaism. Of trying to guide their children to marry into the "right" families (other Converso families) without saying too much about why they cared.

And they were more than just alive. They were right here. In New Mexico and in other parts of the United States, of the world, in fact. The first Converso I actually met face to face, although she would not permit me to interview her, lived in Chicago. If you could find them, you might be able to talk to them, even now. So when I bumped my head against a temporary wall with the Chinese translators, when one of them tried to tell me there was no way peasant women in China could have written poetry, when I realized my hearing was probably not good enough to discern the tiny tonal differences I would need to hear in order to learn Mandarin on my own, I knew I had to try something different, if only for a while as I adjusted my thinking to the new reality of the Chinese story. I just opened my eyes on a bright New Mexico morning and said to myself: why are you making things so difficult when you have interesting people with interesting stories to tell right in your own backyard?

Ahhhh, the innocence of ignorance. After approximately 500 years of living in secret, the Crypto-Jewish community was not about to gather at my feet and start telling me their stories and the stories of their often tormented families. I thought it would be easy because I am Jewish. But I have a very different Jewish background. I learned, eventually, that I would have been able to connect more fully with these people if I were a Spanish-speaking Catholic. We would have had much more in common. I had to learn how to talk to them. I had to learn how to listen. And this I set out to do with the help of two rabbis and one historian in New Mexico. The Nu Shu ladies slipped into the background for a while as this new intrigue consumed me.

CHAPTER SEVEN

I WANTED TO KNOW how the Conversos passed their secret down through the generations, and why some still keep the secret today. I had read several articles on the subject and saw that three people were frequently quoted. One was an Albuquerque Rabbi who is now deceased, another was a Rabbi who lived in Albuquerque at that time, but left some years ago. The third was Dr. Stanley Hordes, a former State Historian of New Mexico with a background in Crypto-Jewish studies and an interest in this part of New Mexico history.

All three clearly had close connections with the Converso community in New Mexico. (I'm using the term Converso since it's all-inclusive. Whether a person is a true Crypto-Jew practicing Judaism in secret while openly Christian, or someone who knows little or nothing of her family's Jewish history, she is still, as a descendant of a Converso, considered a Converso herself.) I approached one Rabbi and told him I was working on a project and wanted to interview Crypto-Jewish women. He said he didn't know any. I knew that wasn't true from the many articles I'd read in which he had been quoted on the subject. He recommended I call the other Rabbi. I did and received the same answer from her. I knew both rabbis were being less than totally honest, but I had no idea why. Of course I understand completely now. They were protecting the community from someone who might come in and expose and exploit them. It had happened before. I was still so early in my research that I didn't understand the nature of the secrecy and the importance to many of these people of keeping the secret. In fact, at my level of understanding I might, indeed, have exposed them, though not meaning to. But the second Rabbi gave me a lead. She sent me to Dr. Hordes.

He took pity on me. Or saw that I was serious and just needed a little guidance. He explained the psychology of the type of research I was proposing. He told me there would be resistance, that I would have to get to know the community slowly, gain their trust; that they were savvy, had been taken advantage of plenty, and that the trust would have to be earned and my sincerity would have to be genuine.

It was all new to me. Nothing like the Nu Shu ladies, who were almost all gone before I came on the scene, and who spoke a foreign language and lived very far away in a very foreign culture. The Conversos were right here in New Mexico. I knew some already, though I wasn't aware that some of the people I was meeting in my everyday life in New Mexico were actually Conversos.

At this point a more complete definition of Converso, Crypto-Jew, and a couple other relevant terms is in order. When I first started my research I thought the two terms were interchangeable, but actually there is a subtle difference. Converso, as I've said, is the Spanish word for convert. Anyone who was converted to Christianity during the Inquisition, whether by choice or by force, is a Converso, and any descendant of such a person is also a Converso. Historians estimate that about forty percent of the original Spanish settlers in the American Southwest, particularly the conquistadores, were Conversos, along for the ride as a way of escaping the long arm of the Inquisition. In some cases, even these early Conversos may have already lost track of their Jewish heritage, or knew and didn't care. Obviously many of their descendants today have no knowledge of their background; others may know their family was Jewish hundreds of years ago but don't incorporate this knowledge into their daily lives; still others know the story and even retain a few Jewish practices, such as lighting candles on Friday night or not eating pork, but consider themselves to be Christians.

In order to be considered a Crypto-Jew, a person has to be outwardly practicing some other religion – most often Catholicism, but some are Protestants – and secretly practicing Judaism and be aware of the reason he or she is doing it. Probably not more than about five percent of all Conversos are actually Crypto-Jews, though there's no way to get an actual count since those are the people who are not telling. The distinction between the two terms is subtle and many people call themselves Crypto-Jews when they may not have been knowingly practicing Judaism in secret. Sometimes members of their families have, but they didn't know it. It's very complicated and fluid and no one should be called out for using the wrong terms.

The word Marrano is well-known but has fallen out of favor

since it means pig or swine. It was originally applied to Conversos by Jews who had resisted conversion and thought that their co-religionists had taken the easy way out. The official term for the converts – the label given to them by the Inquisition – was New Christian, which reflects that they were not truly accepted by the religion they converted to. Technically, they were to remain New Christians for three generations, but often the name continued to be applied as long as anyone could remember that the family had once been Jewish. Currently, the term *Anusim* is favored by Conversos. It is a Hebrew word, a very strong word, which means the forced ones. Conversos feel this more accurately reflects the fact that, for most, the conversion was forced even if their ancestors had appeared to be making the change willingly.

With such subtle differences, there is plenty of room for debate and all Conversos do not see their history in the same way. So discussion has to be approached gingerly; all are definitely not of one mind as to how open a Converso should be. Individuals worry about offending family members who might want to reveal less than they do. They often remain silent more to protect the family secret than because they are truly afraid of persecution. The level of fear that still existed about revealing a Jewish background was amazing to me. It was not until I had spoken to many people that I began to understand that hundreds of years of being told it is not safe to be Jewish does not disappear just because most of us think we live in a "free" country. The current atmosphere of hostility toward minorities in the United States demonstrates that a return of widespread anti-Semitism can happen.

I have interviewed more than 50 individuals and families at this point. The stories of how they found out their histories are all different. Their reactions to the information, when they get it, are just as varied. More than a few have some emotional problems, probably resulting from keeping a secret for so long, if not actually living a double life. I learned to speak very carefully to them. Sometimes it took several meetings before I could begin to ask personal questions.

One woman began to talk to me and then said she couldn't go on because she was picking up a bad vibe from me. I didn't doubt it. It was an early interview and I was pretty nervous because she was a faith healer and seemed fairly eccentric. I said good-by and left. Three months later she called and said she was ready to talk. We talked, then, for several hours and it was clear that she and her family had many Jewish practices and that she knew her history and wanted to learn more. She was learning Hebrew. She was collecting songs in Ladino. (This is Medieval Spanish, also called Judeo-Spanish, which contains elements of Spanish, Hebrew, Arabic, and words from the country in which it was spoken. Many Jews had carried Ladino with them and maintained it in their isolated villages in Mexico and the American Southwest, as well as other parts of the world to which they traveled. While they were living in these outposts, Spanish was evolving and changing elsewhere.) She was incorporating more and more Jewish practices into her life.

At the end of our talk I asked her if she considered herself to be

Jewish. Her jaw dropped and she stared at me for a moment. She stood up and motioned as if to show me the door. "I am Catholic," she said. The interview was over.

CHAPTER EIGHT

GETTING INTERVIEWS did not come naturally for me. Nor was listening to stories a part of my growing up. My mother was definitely *not* a story teller. As a writer, I've always been jealous of other writers who tell in their memoirs how they sat with their families and listened to fabulous stories of the adventures of relatives and neighbors. The great Eudora Welty, for instance, says in her memoir, *One Writer's Beginnings*, that she used to settle in between her mother and her mother's friend in the backseat of their car for a Sunday afternoon ride and say, "Now *talk*." The italics are hers.

Not in my family. To my people everything interesting was a secret.

My grandmother, in a moment of wild abandon I suspect, once told me that two couples I knew – distant cousins, I think – once exchanged partners for one night, as she put it. But would she tell me who? No. She took that secret to her grave.

And then there were the horrible stories. The stories of relatives lost in the Holocaust. That secrecy I have come to understand. Lately the idea is to tell the stories, so we never forget. But I think in the forties and fifties it was just too close. It's one thing to know a lot of people died, even that some relatives you never saw were killed. But to know that your own parents, your brothers and sisters, were rounded up like dogs, subjected to inhuman cruelties, packed into railroad cars like animals, stripped and sent to their deaths in gas chambers, must have been not only profoundly sad, but humiliating as well. Could you tell a ten-year-old granddaughter, sitting at your knee as you bake bread in your warm kitchen, that this had happened to her great grandparents and great aunts and uncles? The standard answer, if I pressed about a particular person, was "Hitler got him." Now, as a mother and grandmother, I understand this silence. I don't remember what I thought at the time. I guess I just accepted it.

Of my mother's stories I heard very few. I know she worked as an order taker for the Montgomery Ward catalog warehouse and that she collected items from the shelves while zipping around on roller skates. This is hard for me to picture because I cannot remember ever seeing her doing anything even remotely athletic. But this is what she said she did. I also know that she was fired from a job for asking for the day off to observe the holiest of Jewish holidays, Yom Kippur. Was it the same job? I don't know. I know she met my father when she was fixed up on a date with him by a cousin of hers who was a friend of my father. I don't know where they went on their first date, only that they were married three years later.

And of my father's life I know even less. He left college after one semester because he was needed to help support his family. He was the oldest of three sons and it was during the Depression. He finally returned to college after retiring and graduated with a Bachelor's degree at the age of 78. What was wrong with me, I often ask myself, that I didn't get more information from them, more stories? But they weren't story tellers. Maybe they never had time. Or were too shy to speak of themselves and their past. I don't know exactly what it was.

My mother's parents, both of whom I loved, did not speak to each other in all the time I knew them. They'd had a fight about something before I was born and never spoke again. What could have been so big a deal that they stopped talking forever while continuing to live together in the same home? I have no idea. No one ever said. No one ever talked about the fact that they didn't speak to each other. Each of their grandchildren noticed it on his or her own, in their own time. Most were in their teens before it dawned on them that these two people never sat next to each other at a gathering and never exchanged a word or a look. I noticed it fairly early on when my grandfather leaned over to me at dinner one night and whispered, "Ask the old lady to pass the salt." I looked to see where the salt was. It was in front of my grandmother. She'd heard him despite the whisper and pushed the salt across the table so I didn't have to ask. I once mentioned to a cousin when we were both around ten years old that our grandparents never spoke to each other. "They don't?" she asked.

They were the kindest of people. But they'd fallen out of love somewhere along the way in their 60-plus years of marriage and they couldn't find their way back. Only in such a silent family could a feud like this go on for decades with no one attempting a reconciliation, or even acknowledging a problem.

So where did my story telling come from? What made me want to be a writer and, later, to record other people's stories? I'd always wanted to be a writer, maybe because there were so many books in our house. Maybe I thought writing that mystery when I was eight would please my parents, who were largely indifferent to our accomplishments but who surely could not ignore a child who wrote a book. They could, though, as it turned out. Later, when I became a published writer, they pretty much ignored that. I can't remember them commenting on any story of mine that appeared in the paper. And my mother was never a great cheerleader for my literary aspirations. When, at the age of 12, I received a diary as a gift she cautioned, "Don't ever write anything in it. You'll be ashamed later."

Telling other people's stories may have been my defense against that risk. The only problem there is you must work up the courage to ask people to talk to you. And then you often must ask them personal questions, also not easy. And, to complicate matters, I chose subjects who were either long gone from the world or were keeping secrets, or both. With the Chinese writers of Nu Shu I could talk to people who had done translations, and do some original research to fill in the blanks. As for the women pioneer diaries there was more information available than I could digest in many years of reading.

But the Converso population presented a real challenge: they were plentiful in number, as documented by historians, but secretive and suspicious and with good reason. Getting interviews was a slow process. On my first visit to the San Felipe de Neri Church in Old Town Albuquerque I met a man I suspected might be a Converso. Dr. Hordes had sent me there, early in my research, to look for two Stars of David somewhere on the walls of the church. I looked all over for something tiny, and then saw them, quite large actually, affixed to the wall on either side and slightly above the altar. They were tilted at an odd angle and had something red inside them, which I later learned were depictions of the sacred heart of Jesus.

This man in the church saw me looking at the stars and offered to tell me their origin. I knew six-pointed stars can be symbols of all sorts of things and that many can be found in churches all through Europe and elsewhere, so I wasn't even sure these were the symbols I was supposed to be looking for. But this man told me that they had been put there by the people who originally built the church, completed in 1711, to remind themselves that although they were Catholic, their origins were Jewish and they did not want to forget that part of their history. The sacred hearts of Jesus had been added during a renovation, less than a hundred years ago. The priest at that time wanted to remove the Stars of David but the community – still largely Converso – did not want the symbols removed. The hearts inside the stars were a compromise.

The man said he had been baptized in this church but that an aunt of his had been Jewish and he'd learned many things about the

Jewish religion from her. I was sure at that point that he was a Converso, but I didn't want to push it. I was learning to take it easy. I returned to the Church many times over the next couple years. Every time, the same man was there. He had appointed himself a sort of informal docent, it seemed, and he told me something new about the history of the community each time I spoke with him. He also let me know, at one point, that his uncle had been Jewish. Finally, he admitted that his parents had been, as he put it, "a little bit Jewish." I had my opening at last. "Wouldn't that make you a little bit Jewish?" I asked. "I guess it would," he said.

It was such a simple acknowledgement. He said those words – in that way – because at that point he trusted me. I continued to visit him at the Church for several years but I already knew all I needed to know about him and his family. I know his name but he is no longer with us and never gave me permission to use it so I will not reveal it here. Longtime residents of the community would be able to guess but they most certainly would know his Converso background already.

CHAPTER NINE

I'D NOT BEEN FED on the notion that writing was a thing to aspire to, indeed that it could be a career or even a likely avocation. In the fourth grade I'd had a teacher who told my mother that she envisioned me as a writer when I grew up. Surprisingly, my mother reported this to me and I think, at that point, my fate was sealed. When I was in eighth grade, maybe seventh – I'm not sure – I entered a contest sponsored by a local bank. It was to write an essay about why I was proud to be an American, or something like that. The prize was a trip to Washington, D.C., and a U.S. Savings Bond. I came in second place. Later I learned that the daughter of the president of the bank had come in first place. I learned a lot that day. I would have loved to have seen her essay.

All through my school years I'd been considered a "good" writer, whatever that means. I think at the time it meant I didn't make any grammatical errors. Later, when I started writing for the *Chicago Tribune*, one of my editors confirmed that that was truly a skill to be proud of. "Listen, kid," he said, (I think I was older than he was, but never mind, that's how I remember it) "the easier the editing job for me, the more work you get. And so far it's been a breeze working with your stuff." Whoopty do! I was a good writer. Truth is, if you could honor a deadline and turn in fairly clean copy you were in. Adequacy was the primary requirement. I filled the bill and then some, but the "then some" wasn't worth anything extra as far as pay was concerned. And if I balked at that, I could be replaced by someone who was just adequate. They didn't need the "then some" and I knew it. I was, of course, freelance, which accounted for my low status. The staff writers I knew all earned – and deserved – more respect.

So how can you excel at newspaper writing if you're on a low rung of the ladder? Well, you can still get the great story. The unusual, the heartbreaking, the scandalous, the heartwarming. I quickly learned that nobody can take that away from you. I did that: women coping with having babies in prison, immigrants adjusting to life in Chicago, young folks following in the footsteps of their parents' careers, and all that that entails and, not the least, Chinese women figuring out a secret writing system they could embroider into table cloths to get messages back to their sisters and friends at home.

And I could learn – on my own, I might add – how to get a good interview. How to find the people, how to get them to talk, how to ask the right questions to get at the true story. And how to listen. I say I learned all this on my own, because I never took any courses in journalism. And I never told any of my editors that I hadn't studied journalism formally, so I was always afraid to ask a question that might turn out to be something I should have learned on the first day of my non-existent journalism education. I have to admit there was a bit of trial and error involved, especially in the beginning.

I tried to make friends with other writers and learn from them the secrets of how to find famous people willing to be interviewed. Oh, it was easy enough when they had a book or movie coming out. Then they came to you, with a free book for you into the bargain. But the rest of the time forget it. They had no reason to talk to me.

I wrote a regular column for several years called Chicago Voices. It could be about anybody, the hook on every story being that they lived in Chicago or, usually even more interesting because readers didn't always know this, that they used to live in Chicago when they were kids or at some time in the past. The subjects ranged from fairly well-known to very famous. But if they weren't plugging a product it was really tough to get them. For instance, Oprah, back in the days before she was really famous and was mainly known only in Chicago, would never talk to me. She turned me down a couple times as her popularity steadily increased on a national level, and finally I had to admit that she had attained a high enough status that if she ever wanted publicity she wasn't going to have to go to my little column to get it.

I started the column in 1989 with the likes of jazz pianist Ramsey Lewis, singer Lou Rawls, and the ballet star Maria Tallchief. I interviewed the *Cheers* actor George Wendt, Adlai Stevenson III (the son of the Presidential candidate, who was then a former Illinois Governor), jazz vocalist Mel Torme, the "velvet fog," actor Mandy Patinkin, Donald Rumsfeld, Secretary of Defense under Presidents Gerald Ford and the younger George Bush. I talked to

Clayton Moore, better known as the Lone Ranger, the Watergate reporter Bob Woodward, the film director William Friedkin, the Chicago lawyer and mystery writer Scott Turow. All lived or had lived in Chicago. I sat next to actor John Mahoney on the couch in his living room in suburban Oak Park and tried my best not to swoon. He was just a plain, old-fashioned nice man. I talked to dozens of people known only to Chicagoans. The column finally ended its run in 1993 with my interview of Hugh Hefner. Don't ask.

I say that because there's really nothing much to tell. We did the interview over the phone. Hefner was extremely intelligent and couldn't have been kinder, friendlier or more personable if he tried. As we talked I imagined what he might be picturing in terms of the appearance of this unknown reporter. I tried not to let on that I was not very much younger than he and wondered if he was picturing a Playboy Bunny type at the other end of the call.

The "getting," as they say, of each of these people is a story in itself. Here's one example: I did an interview with Debbie Reynolds in 1991 after she wrote a book about her life. I mentioned, when I turned in the story, that we'd had a good time together, and the story turned out well. So my editor thought I might have some luck using my acquaintance with Reynolds to get to her daughter, Carrie Fisher, who played Princess Leia in *Star Wars*. She hadn't done anything of note just before this time, and therefore was impossible to "get."

I began immediately by contacting Reynolds. She was most encouraging and said she'd pass the word on to Carrie's publicist.

Several months and several phone calls later, it still hadn't happened. Ms. Fisher was out of the country. Ms. Fisher was busy with projects. And so on. Then one day, a full five months after I'd first met her mother, Carrie Fisher's assistant called to tell me Carrie could give me one hour if I'd call back in five minutes. Yes, of course, and after five mad minutes of hustling about my office looking for notes I'd made months earlier, paper, pencils, tape recorder and anything else I could think of that I might need, I made the call and was put through to Ms. Fisher. Who seemed ill. Who seemed distracted. Who couldn't speak two words without gasping for air.

There was a little clicking sound in the background (I was listening!) and as the conversation progressed and I started to feel more comfortable, I was able to put two and two together and suddenly knew what was happening. Ms. Fisher was on an exercise machine of some sort. Maybe her television wasn't working or her trainer hadn't shown up. For whatever reason, it suited her needs to use me as a companion while she did her workout. It was not much of an ego-soother for me, but I got the interview and wrote the story and in the end liked her very much, once I unruffled my feathers.

One assignment that I didn't have to "get" was interviewing long-time, and very well-known, advice columnist Ann Landers, Eppie Lederer in real life. This one was handed to me. Assigned by one of my editors. I jumped at it. I'd always read her column and thought it would be a hoot to meet her. It wasn't.

I interviewed her in her home just off Michigan Avenue, the famous Magnificent Mile in Chicago. What a scoop I could have had but I decided to protect her instead. And she wasn't even nice to me. She had slipped and said something revealing that she shouldn't have said. It was just a couple words but I knew what they meant. And she knew I knew. She even knew I knew she knew. If you can follow that. But I just couldn't do it. I could see she was scared. So I didn't include it in the story and I never told anyone. And I never will. That's why I'm an unknown journalist and not a famous one. But relatively happy and at peace with myself, for whatever that's worth. Plenty.

CHAPTER TEN

THROUGHOUT THE 1980S AND 1990S and well into the new century, I continued to write newspaper articles as well as study my three larger interests: the writers of Nu Shu, Conversos, and American women's pioneer diaries. There were some similarities between the Chinese women and the American women, in particular, but few pioneer women suffered the extensive abuse that was fairly common among the Nu Shu ladies. There were pioneer women who told of escaping from abusive husbands, and others who told stories of being kidnapped by various Native peoples. Some escaped their captors or were rescued by their families or, in some cases, by the United States Army. But many chose to stay with a tribe where they felt comfortable, sometimes because they had fallen in love with one of the men of that tribe. In the nineteenth century, several women earned their living on the lecture circuit telling the story of their experiences living with "the Natives."

Some of the pioneer diaries were written by very young girls, often as young as thirteen. Like their mothers, aunts, or older sisters – or grandmothers, for that matter – they were along on the trip because of a man: father, brother, even a son or sons. Still, they put their hearts into it and did the lion's share of the work. They cooked, they kept track of the animals and took care of the small children. They mended clothes, they tended the sick and dying, they delivered babies. Some of them produced surprisingly good writing in their diaries or letters home, considering that they often had limited education; much of it was laced with very mature insights for teenage girls.

I think my favorite is Virginia Reed. She and her family were a part of the ill-fated Donner Party, which left Missouri for California in May, 1846, followed a poorly charted route called the Hastings Cutoff, and got trapped in an unexpected early snowfall in what is now known as Donner Pass in the Sierra Nevada. The group had to turn to cannibalism to survive. Virginia Reed was only thirteen at the time, though she lived into her nineties, and always maintained that her family had never resorted to eating human flesh. She tells the story in a very cogent manner in a letter to a cousin. After detailing some of their wrong decisions, such as taking a trail that they thought would be a shortcut, and leaving too late and encountering the weather which trapped them in the pass, she closes the letter to her cousin with the advice that she should always hurry along and "don't take no shortcuts." An understatement if ever there was one. Also a message you can take anywhere; trot it out and it will always be appropriate.

There was no question of escape from nasty husbands or bad family situations with the Nu Shu ladies. A woman simply could not live alone in China in those times. In fact, no matter how horrible a woman's marriage was, divorce was virtually unknown and it was a far worse fate than a bad marriage to become a widow, especially if her children were still young and could not support her. Then she was at the mercy of her husband's family, which may have been hateful to her for as long as she had known them. Sometimes they took her children away from her. And most of the time she was not allowed to remarry even though that would have helped the situation considerably. One daughter spoke of the disgrace her widowed mother brought to the family by remarrying and how she refused to speak to her mother afterward.

Not surprisingly, I can see now, looking back, there are connections to my own life in some of these stories. My maternal grandmother, for instance, could not divorce her husband when she thought (maybe only for a brief time) that she wanted to in 1954 in the United States. They had not spoken, as I've said, for longer than I'd been alive, which that summer was twelve years. I don't know what led to that break in communication, but in the summer of that year I overheard her telling my mother she would like to get a divorce.

My mother's reply: "Absolutely not. It's a disgrace."

The idea was that families like ours – what did that mean? Upstanding? Intelligent? Respectable? I really have no idea – didn't have divorces. Though of course they did. Even then I knew of a cousin of my mother who was married to a second wife, though the existence of the first marriage was supposed to be a secret.

My mother prevailed. My grandmother was an immigrant. She was literate and very smart, but maybe she didn't know how to go about getting a lawyer. Maybe. More likely she just bowed to my mother's pressure. Or decided against divorce on her own. My mother, to her credit, did not just ignore the situation. She suggested a cooling-off period for her parents in which my grandmother would visit relatives in Los Angeles for five weeks with guess who in tow to give an excuse for the trip: me.

I, of course, was not supposed to know the reason for the trip. But I did. We flew on a plane – seven hours in those days – and I was sick all the way. Perhaps that was the point of my presence because my propensity toward motion sickness was well-known. Anyway, the beginning of my grandmother's liberation was probably not all she'd hoped it would be. But she loved me and put up with it without complaint and we had the time of our lives in Los Angeles. At least I did. We stayed with my other grandmother, my father's mother, and the two of them spent the whole time each trying to prove she was more devoted to me than the other. They took me to movies and dueled it out in the kitchen. One was an excellent baker. The other made the best soups and chicken and fish dishes. I ate like royalty, my every whim indulged. Since I was not accustomed to coddling, pampering, or being shown a good time in my regular life at home in Chicago, this was easily the highlight of my childhood.

Besides the attention from my grandmothers, I was exposed to a bunch of cousins I barely knew before, all of whom were allowed more privileges than I had ever dreamed of. The best one – or so it seemed to me living with the strict bedtime hours my parents imposed – was staying up late at night. Neither of my two summer guardians wanted to be the one to say no, so I just did whatever I wanted. I'd call this time the most normal period in my childhood, short as it was. I can't say what it did for my grandparents' marriage; they continued the silent treatment to the end of their lives. Still, there was no more talk of divorce that I ever heard.

A couple of times in my own marriage when life seemed to overwhelm me – work, kids, a husband with his own absorbing career and little sympathy for my stresses – I took off for California and a visit with my aunt and uncle. I couldn't have told you why I did it, but it helped. No doubt I was unthinkingly following a message I'd received as a child: divorce is out of the question; take a break in a place that's freer and more fun. Whether it did any more for me than it did for my grandmother I couldn't say. I feel for the Nu Shu ladies who never had the chance to just get away for a while. And the pioneer women? Well, they were headed for California and other Western spots too but, alas, not for fun and freedom. Life in the West was hard as they planted and built and learned to live in a very different environment.

CHAPTER ELEVEN

My own connection to the Nu Shu ladies, to the pioneer women, even to the Crypto-Jewish women eluded me at first. They all had in common that they found ways to tell their stories against all odds. The Nu Shu ladies invented a streamlined writing system that could be embroidered into textiles of all sorts. The pioneer women wrote at the end of busy days filled with hard labor and bitter disappointment. Then they had to protect their journals from being tossed out to lighten the load if their family lost a wagon to an accident or breakdown and had to consolidate their possessions. The Crypto-Jewish women passed on their family stories, religious prayers, and rituals, such as they could remember, for generations by telling their daughters and imploring them to divulge the secret only to the right people. Most of it was shared orally, but I have found some journals written by these women.

But what about me? I've always had the tools I needed for expanding my writing to include my own stories and, let's face it, enough time if I only tried to find it. I never had encouragement but neither did any of these women and it didn't stop them. It seems what I didn't have is guts. The guts to tell the truth. The guts to get past the fear of hurting someone's feelings or, dare I say it, making someone angry at me. I was already writing at the age of eight. I wanted to write. But I gravitated to other people's stories, once I was able to access them through newspaper writing. My own? They were largely unknown to me still.

So I get these women. I know how it feels to want to tell your story. I understand the need to write. And from these women I've learned the benefits of writing, not only for the writer, but for the readers, too, who can learn so much. All these women opened windows into their culture that the largely male historians, until modern times, never could have opened. The women writers told us about aspects of life in their homes that men might have rejected, or wouldn't have noticed, or wouldn't have thought important if they did notice. And they provided emotional support for each other while they did so. The Nu Shu writers, in particular, became a sisterhood as children, and remained so throughout their lives because they could record and share their stories. For them this was probably the biggest benefit of all.

It seems women always find ways to do that. It doesn't have to be through writing. They get together in all sorts of groups and talk about books or gossip about their neighbors or discuss politics. But writing adds an extra dimension, I think, because it lasts. They can look back on it later and see what they've accomplished. And others can benefit from the stories told or written. They provide an education to the reader, whether it is an old friend being filled in on the news from the next village, or an unknown and unimagined reader in the future learning something about life in a distant place and time.

I think of my own mother who led a rather sheltered and, I suspect, lonely life. She did not have a group of women friends that she met with. She didn't drive and didn't even go grocery shopping without my father. For a twentieth century woman, she had less of an outlet and less of a support system than the Nu Shu ladies had. One of my strongest memories from childhood is a picture, in my mind, of my brother, David, and myself sitting on our mother's lap. My brother is two; I am five. We are the first of the five children my mother would eventually have and raise. My mother is wearing one of those aprons that cover the whole dress, with ruffles over the shoulders. Think of the sitcoms of the 1950's: *Leave it to Beaver. Father Knows Best.* (Even with aprons, the mom usually wore pearls and high heels.) My mother is amply built, in this picture in my memory, but not what you would call heavy. From pictures, I know that my mother was very slim when she married and had probably gained about thirty pounds by her first anniversary. Then she started having children and just stayed a little overweight for the rest of her life.

In my memory it feels like morning, but I can't be sure. We are sitting on her lap, looking at each other and she is crying. Tears are coming out of her beautiful blue eyes and running down her face. I don't know what happened before that moment, or after, to tell the truth. It is a photo in my mind. I don't know why she is crying, when she started, when she stopped, or whether David and I had any reaction to it. But I have remembered that picture all my life. I believe it was so disturbing to me, as a child, that it served as a guiding principle to me in raising my own children. I always wanted them to believe that everything was all right. Never let them see you cry.

So now I have had the guts to tell that little story. I must be the only one alive who knows it. David was only two and says he doesn't remember. If he did, it would probably be a different memory from mine, given his age. And, of course, viewed from the other side of her lap. Who knows?

But it is a story, not sketched hastily into a journal written at the end of a long day's arduous journey. Not embroidered into someone's foot binding cloth. Not whispered to a daughter. No, this one is written down late in life. For what? To preserve it? To release it? To provide a window into a mid-twentieth century home that may or may not have been like many others? I think all of the above, all are the answers as well as the questions. This is part of what I know from the women who write – or just embroider or whisper if they have to – that the stories are the questions *and* the answers. And on it goes.

To the best of my knowledge my mother only made one attempt at independence during her married life. My father did not believe that married women should work outside the home. He felt that would make the husband appear unable to support his family. When I, his oldest child, got married at the age of twenty-one he thought I should quit teaching. This was in 1965, so his ideas had not changed in the quarter century of living since his own marriage. He was well-meaning but incredibly stubborn.

His view of women's subordination to men extended to the automobile as well. He didn't think women should drive cars. Among other things, he didn't want to have to adjust the rear-view mirror in his car after someone else drove it. He wouldn't let me learn to drive and I didn't until I was twenty and my boyfriend, who was soon to become my husband (and who didn't want a wife who couldn't drive), taught me. Naturally, my father wouldn't let my mother learn to drive a car. This little issue was exacerbated by the fact that in the fifties he had a job that took him out of town for two weeks out of every month. We were three children by that time and when my father was out of town our car sat, untouched, in front of our house. If my mother needed to shop or take a child to the doctor she had to call a neighbor or relative to drive us.

My mother's sole source of income was whatever my father doled out to her when she asked him for money. Somehow, over a period of time that I can't even fathom, she saved enough money for driving lessons and she took them whenever my father was out of town. (I have a dim recollection that they cost eight dollars each, which would have been quite a bit at that time, especially for a woman of no means.) She even took the driving test and got her license without telling him. Then came the moment of truth. One day when my father returned from a two-week trip she showed him her driver's license. Her subjugation to him was such that she wouldn't have dared to drive the car without his permission. It's doubtful she even had a key for the car. My father's reaction was predictable: he was livid.

He announced that she would have to pass *his* test before he would let her touch his car. They bundled all three of us kids into the back seat and my mother got behind the wheel and my father climbed in beside her. To my ten-year-old eyes it was the most unusual sight I'd ever seen. My mother the driver and my father the passenger. I'll never forget it and, as you can probably guess, it's a sight I never saw again.

My father began to give instructions: Pull out of the space; turn the wheel this way; turn it that way; slow down; be careful. As we approached the end of the block he said "turn." And my mother turned. Right on to the sidewalk. My father burst out laughing. "Women can't drive cars," he said. He opened his door and got out. She opened hers and got out. They changed places. He turned the car around and drove us back home. No one ever said another word about it. My mother never got behind the wheel of a car again, but she renewed her driver's license whenever it came due and received a commendation from the state for a safe driving record each time. Many, many years later, when the wounds – maybe – were healed, she used to joke about her perfect record. Did she cry by herself? I wonder.

This may be my favorite story about my mother, not because of what happened when she tried to drive for my father, but because of the spunk she showed in learning to drive on her own. It is a memory that only I have. My parents are both gone and my brothers don't remember. David was seven and Alan only four when it happened. Also, being boys, they may not have identified with her and the driving issue the way I did. But it is one of the strongest memories from my childhood.

My mother was crestfallen. She looked totally humiliated. I can't even imagine how I would have felt after going through what she did only to be beaten down like that in front of all of us. I do not wish to make a villain of my father, though. He was a gentle and generous man. He would never have laid a hand on any of us in anger. He was a kind man who believed in what he thought was the proper way to conduct a life. He would do anything to help anyone. And I'm sure he was shocked by my mother's bold act of independence, which was so out of character for her. The thought of her taking those driving lessons behind his back would certainly have been enough to make him lose his usual cool demeanor. To his credit, he did eventually change some of his views along with the changing times. (Among other things he accepted that both my sister – who was not even born yet when this incident took place – and I had jobs and drove cars.) But on that day, the hard line he took surely killed my mother's spirit.

The dynamic between my mother and father was and still is a mystery to me. For much of my childhood and adult life I was angry with her, probably because she was very critical of me. It wasn't until she was diagnosed with dementia and I realized that she'd already had it an awfully long time, and may have had some mental disorder for as long as I'd known her, that I began to soften toward her. And it was only when I was able to step back from my anger that I saw that she'd been depressed. Depressed and repressed.

Misunderstood. That her sharp tongue and judgmental attitude, her negativity, may not have come from meanness of spirit, as I'd assumed, but from frustration at not being able to make any choices for herself, and maybe sadness and loneliness, too.

Now what I feel for her is sympathy. At this late date. Too late.

CHAPTER TWELVE

WHAT HAPPENS TO THE STORIES we don't tell? Do they just go away? I don't believe so. Do they settle into a corner of the brain and wait to come out in dreams and nightmares? Do they scream for freedom and keep hammering and digging until they make a tunnel and escape? One way or another they are a burden – it is always a burden to keep a secret – if they are not released. We must continue to support them, like lifers in prison, no hope for parole or release. Just keep feeding them and they'll stay alive but in a shadow existence, not really part of the fabric of life but not erasable either.

The Nu Shu ladies did not let that happen to their stories. There was the young bride who just wanted to take a present to her mother for her fortieth birthday. She was beaten by her mother-in-law because she attempted the journey of two miles to her family home on her own. But she is remembered. Because she told her story. Yes, she had to sew it into a tablecloth. And, yes, maybe no one knew the story during her lifetime. But someone knows it now. I know it. The women in Taipei who translated the story into Mandarin know it. The Tai Chi instructor in Chicago who translated the story from Mandarin into halting English for me knows it. Even if that is the end of it, it is better than nothing. It is better than being a lifer with no hope of escape. Just to tell the story releases it into the world. For people to learn from it. And for the writer to exist forever, to not have her life erased. Finally, I did put it into a book so maybe even more people will know her story. Details on that adventure later.

Even little stories tell so much. My paternal grandmother's love of "machines," for instance. My grandmother called everything that moved or made a noise a machine. The radio was a machine and later, so was the television. The telephone was a machine you could use to summon people. The electric toaster was a machine. The record player was a music machine.

But her favorite machine was the car. She loved to take a ride in the machine on a Sunday, but she was deathly afraid that the doors would pop open while the machine was in motion and someone – no doubt a helpless child – would be tossed out. In fact, she knew of such an incident and it was an elderly lady who fell out on the highway and was then run over by a car and killed. Or so she said.

So even before my father could turn the key and start the motor of the machine, everyone had to check his door and announce that it was locked. (No seatbelts, of course, back in the day.) Then we could take off. But we could not drive too fast in the machine. Grandma became queasy if the machine rocked too vigorously. My mother always let her sit in front so the motion wouldn't be too much for her, but it didn't help.

What sitting in front did do, was give her a clear view of the road and a chance to do a little of what we called backseat driving, which drove my father crazy. She'd read, in all seriousness, the street signs aloud and say something like, "Twenty-five miles per hour. How do you like that?" Or "No right turn. You don't say." This, she must have felt, did not sound so much like she was instructing him. Later, when my father was her age and she was long gone, he did the same thing to me.

My father, of course, was more modern, but there was one machine he didn't like and that was the television. He didn't think it was going anywhere. He thought it was a complete waste of time. Well, almost complete. He approved of the puppet show *Kukla, Fran and Ollie*. He approved of *Stud's Place*, a very early program in which the Chicago author, Studs Terkel, was the main character, a bartender I think, but I'm not sure. Those were either local Chicago shows, or started in Chicago and moved out to the rest of the country. He liked *Your Show of Shows*, a comedy offering with Sid Caesar, among others, and the *Ed Sullivan Show*. He would not let us watch *I Love Lucy* and he thought *Howdy Doody* "taught children bad things."

Our only hope for watching a little television was on Saturday mornings when he was working. My mother could be talked into most things as long as she felt it was absolutely certain my father wouldn't find out. It was our little secret. So David and Alan and I would watch old Laurel and Hardy movies and *Felix the Cat* cartoons and laugh our heads off. We thought they were hysterical. (Please remember there weren't many kids' programs to choose from in those days.) I can still sing the song for Felix: "Felix the cat/

the wonderful, wonderful cat/ Whenever he gets in a fix/ he reaches into his bag of tricks."

We also watched something called *Hair Raising Tale*. It was a half hour commercial for some hair product, a precursor to the modern-day infomercial, I guess. The name of the company was something like Charles Antel. It was exactly the same every week, showing that a paper curled in the solution exactly as a person's hair would. Our clandestine television entertainment ended one Saturday when my father found us talking about something called *Hair Raising Tale*. He was appalled that our mother was letting us watch horror movies. We tried to explain but to no avail. He would not believe it was a commercial for a hair curling product. Our secret Saturday morning entertainment vice was over forever and our mother was scorned for lazy parenting.

A bigger problem, for me if not for my brothers, was that we weren't allowed to watch *I Love Lucy*. You can't imagine what I went through on Tuesday mornings to cover up that I hadn't seen America's favorite program the night before. Everyone on our block knew we weren't allowed to watch the show, so that was a lost cause anyway. So on Tuesday morning on the school bus I'd just keep quiet and listen. Then when I'd get to school – I think this was third grade – I could join in the conversation with "wasn't it funny when Lucy . . .?" or some such thing I'd heard on the bus. I don't know if I fooled anybody but what I had going for me was that no one could have imagined that anyone didn't watch that show so maybe they weren't suspicious. For what it's worth, my grown-up self thinks my father was absolutely right. It was a pretty silly program, though now appreciated as a ground-breaking sit-com

CHAPTER THIRTEEN

My mother was not a very good housekeeper. In the sixties and seventies, with the coming of the modern feminist movement, lax housekeeping became almost chic as women turned to loftier goals than keeping up with the dusting. But in the forties and fifties, when I was growing up, poor housekeeping was considered a disgrace, or so it seemed to me. For me it was a great embarrassment because all of my friends' mothers were perfect post-war mommies who cleaned and cooked and did the laundry in a timely fashion. My mother did none of these things. Instead she read – and I have no quarrel with that – and watched television, which my father wouldn't permit when he was home, and generally moped around the house in her bathrobe.

When she did the laundry, the living room sofa was piled half way to the ceiling with clean, dried clothes, neither ironed nor folded nor sorted in any way. It was up to us kids to get our own stuff out of the pile and put it all away. Then, usually when we needed the couch for sitting, she gathered up whatever was left and stashed it somewhere or, as often as not, transferred it to a vacant chair.

Her management of clutter was a mystery to all of us. Items of all sorts were moved from one place to another over a period of months and even years to, as my mother would say, "get them out of the way." So a stapler, for instance, that someone set down on a table might remain on that table for weeks. Then it would be gone, completely out of sight when somebody needed it. And then, several years later, someone might remove a book from the bookcase and there would be the stapler, right behind those books.

One evening in 1965, after we'd been married a couple months, my husband, Gary, and I went over to my parents' house for dinner. "What's this?" Gary asked, holding up an oddly-shaped bottle that was on an old round coffee table, the entire table having been pushed into a corner at some point to get it out of the way. I recognized it immediately. "Oh my," I said, "that's my bottle of Quink." Now Quink, some might remember, was a brand of ink, packaged in an oddly squished, rectangular bottle, the ink to be used in fountain pens in the fifties. I can't have used it past the fifth grade because by then we were into ball point pens. I probably hadn't seen this item in more than a decade. Yet here it was, not hidden away in a trunk in the basement, not even stashed behind some books, but right out in the open where, had it been there at any time during the past decade, it would have been seen by everybody every day, and no one but I even knew what it was. My mother claimed never to have seen it before in her life.

My mother kept up her unorthodox ways of organizing clutter all through her life. About two years before she died, her dementia reached a point where we had to move her from her assisted living apartment to a nursing home. After she was settled in, my brothers,

David and Chuck, and I went back to clean out her apartment. We found that she had spent much of her time organizing old family photographs. She had put 18 or 20 photos each into several plastic food storage containers. Each container had a series of pictures that progressed chronologically from the early 1900's to around 2000, when she must have stopped collecting and arranging the photos. Each container also had one pair of panty hose. The containers were located in cabinets and drawers all over the apartment. Also in the refrigerator. I once asked my mother, years earlier when we were trying to locate an important piece of mail, why she didn't just have one place to put the mail each day when it came so she would not always be losing it. She said, "That's not how my mind works." I guess not.

Also, my mother was not a very good cook. She could not plan ahead so she frequently did not have all the ingredients she needed for a recipe. And since she didn't drive she could not run out to the store to get what she needed. A neighbor might have had what she wanted, but I don't remember her ever borrowing from a neighbor.

"I didn't have lemons," she would explain as she set some dish down on the table, "so I used vanilla. I think it will be all right."

We could never understand her method for choosing the substitute ingredients. Similarity of taste seemed to have nothing to do with it. I had a theory that it was bulk. Whatever would fill up the space in the same way as the missing ingredient was what she used. Or it may have been more random than that – whatever she laid her eyes on first. She did always replace solids with solids and liquids with liquids, so there was that.

And, no, it was never all right. It resulted in some very strange concoctions. You can't use vanilla instead of lemon in a sauce for chicken. Or peanut butter where cream cheese is called for. Or sprinkle raisins on green beans because you don't have slivered almonds.

Whatever I knew about cooking when I got married – not much — I learned from my mother. And this is what I learned: try to plan ahead a little bit.

And when she died (in 2008 – my father had already died in 1999) and we all went to the rabbi to talk about her and give her some suggestions for the eulogy, the rabbi said, "Five children. She must have been a wonderful homemaker." We stared at the floor, sheepishly. No one wanted to say it.

"She must have been quite a cook," she prodded us.

"She was an imaginative cook," I said.

"Really? How delightful. You wouldn't have thought she'd have the time."

"She was an amazing woman," I said. And I guess she was. She was different, in any event.

But back in the fifties, when I was dealing with all the typical struggles of growing up, which mostly boiled down to trying to be like everyone else, my embarrassment about my mother's house-keeping was only a part of my angst.

There was also the struggle to fit in at school. In the fourth grade my teacher was Miss Twitty. I adored that woman even though her ways in the classroom caused me a great deal of anxiety. She was the teacher who told my mother that she thought I was going to be a writer some day and that may have been part of why I liked her despite her misguided teaching practices, as I now see them. She looked like a teacher—fifties style – with her white hair tied into a neat bun at the back of her head. She always wore a black dress. She was old enough to have been allowed to teach without a college degree and the story was that she did not have one. She certainly had no training in any principles of education I know of. She posted all the students' grades on the board for all their work, every day. There were no secrets; everyone knew who was the quickest learner and who was the slowest. For each subject we had different seats with the "smartest" kids in the front of the classroom and the ones having difficulties at the back. I didn't understand the logic of that at the time and I still don't. I have a degree in education and I know I never learned to do anything like that.

Miss Twitty was a stickler for manners. Once she was giving a ruler to a little girl in our class. The girl was standing at Miss Twitty's desk. Miss Twitty had one end of the ruler and my classmate had the other. They were looking at each other. Miss Twitty would not let go. None of us knew why, least of all the child on the other end of the ruler. At last Miss Twitty said, "Say thank you." The little girl did and the ruler was released.

I sat at the back of the room in what was called arithmetic in those days. It was still a year until I was going to learn that I was nearsighted. I could not see the board very well because of my eyesight and because of being so far back. My scores in arithmetic did not improve all year and in one quarter I received a failing grade. But I sat in the front row in reading. I was one of the best readers in the class.

The only exception to this setup was music, where Miss Twitty operated under a reverse strategy. On the first day of school Miss Twitty walked around the classroom while we sang together and put her ear in front of each child's mouth. Those who were singing well were moved to the back of the room so their voices would carry forward and help the others. The worse your voice, the closer to the front you sat. I sat in the front row. I was told I could not carry a tune and that was the first time I'd heard that expression. Eventually I was told to just mouth the words. The message was that even in the front row, my voice was so bad I could do damage to the whole group.

We each had to have a turn playing a song on the piano and singing. Individually. I was terrified. I did not have a piano at home and could not practice. And, of course, I could not sing. That had been documented and announced publicly to the class. One person was to take a turn each week. Miss Twitty advised us to go early if we were nervous. Cowards die many times before their death, she told us. I could never take a turn. The entire school year went by and everyone had a turn except me. I lived a life of fear that whole year. She was certainly correct about the fate of cowards. At the end of the school year I was the only one who had never taken a turn. I loved Miss Twitty for taking pity on me and not making a fuss about it so everyone would notice. But I knew it meant my voice was so bad that she had had to set aside one of her own rules to protect me from myself.

Once that year I did a terrible thing. I tried to strangle my brother Alan. In my defense, he'd done something worthy of retribution. He'd taken the head off my favorite doll, Annabelle. Just pulled it clean off. I came home one day and there she was, sitting in her best dress — she was one of those pre-Barbie dolls that looked like a little toddler — and her head was in her lap. I remember screaming. I knew Alan had to have done it because he was the only one home while David and I were in school.

As it happened my parents were away somewhere and my grandmother was taking care of us for a few days. Since, unlike my mother, she cleaned and cooked when she was at our house, she must have been busy when Alan, only three, was up to this mischief. He was watching from the kitchen when I saw the beheaded Annabelle. I grabbed him, threw him down on the sofa and began to shake him with my hands around his neck. I can't explain this violent reaction. Maybe it was the constant tension of waiting my turn to solo at the piano at school but, anyway, that's what I did. As I remember, it went on for a long time but probably it was only seconds since Alan's screams brought my grandmother into the room immediately. I can still remember the look of horror on her face. I dropped him back onto the sofa before she could even say a word.

For what it's worth I could never have killed him. Oh, Alan, writing this has made me miss you so much. It was ungrateful of me to have attempted murder over such a small infraction in the scheme of things. First you played the baby for us when David and I played house. Then you followed us around like a loyal servant when we came home from school. Later you were the glue that held the family together when there were five siblings, and even after we were all grown up you remembered the birthdays, the holidays, all our special events. You organized when we were disorganized and made everything happen. And you left us so soon. We're not as much without you, either, as we were when you were here. So I'm sorry for scaring you that day. I know you were just bored, maybe angry that David and I weren't home most of the day. I'd give you back Annabelle's head, and anything else you want, to have you with us again.

CHAPTER FOURTEEN

MY SISTER SAYS my mother never drew pictures, but I know she did. I am almost fifteen years older than my sister Rochelle, and my mother was also that much older and not really the same woman that she had been when I was a little girl. Our mother was a 42-year-old woman when Rochelle was born; she had previously had five pregnancies and lost one of the babies at birth. When I was born she was a young girl in her twenties whose new, first baby – me – was a novelty to the whole extended family and apparently adored by all. I probably survived with a few intact marbles because of being that first baby and getting all that extra attention, much more than my mother was able to give the children who followed.

By the time Rochelle was born, my mother didn't have the time to draw pictures. Or the energy. Or the inclination. She was just trying to keep her head above water. But for me she drew funny little doodles, usually with a pencil, of women in high heels and 1940's dresses. She showed me how to draw the high heeled shoes by starting with the number three. I can still do it.

If I had to guess what hurt my mother the most in her life, I would say it was when her fourth baby died at birth. It was not exactly a still birth but it was never completely explained to me. I was eight years old when it happened and I was told my father had

had to choose between my mother's life and the baby's and he chose my mother. I've never known exactly what that means but it seems like the baby was alive at some point. I really don't know.

While we were waiting for the baby to be born I used to say a prayer every night. I had two younger brothers so I prayed every night that the baby would be a girl. I really wanted a sister. The baby was a girl and she died. I thought that God was teaching me a lesson. That I had been selfish in asking for a girl but not asking for her to be healthy. So I got only what I asked for, a sister.

I really think this broke my mother's spirit because, apart from the obvious, that her baby did not survive, we never spoke about it afterwards. (Which is probably why I never learned exactly what happened to the baby.) There was no normal grieving process for any of us. The only thing I ever heard my mother say after she came home from the hospital was, "I told the doctor there was something wrong. The baby wasn't moving anymore. I told him, but he wouldn't listen."

I never saw her cry after she lost this child, but she must have. If she ever talked to me about it I don't remember. She did show me her scar from the cesarean delivery, a much more prominent marking than the modern-day equivalent. I didn't want to see it but she insisted. I don't know why she wanted me to see it. I was just a child and frightened by it but I looked quickly and got away as soon as I could.

I don't know what happened to the baby. Was she buried some-where? I know her name and it wouldn't surprise me if there's no one else who does, except maybe David. Her name was Sarah. If she had a middle name I don't know it. There is never any remembrance of the day she died. It was June 22, 1952. This is the same date as my brother Alan's death, many years later. My mother lost two of her six children on June 22, and it was she who reminded me of the date the baby died and of the coincidence of Alan and the baby both dying on the same date.

The next time my mother was pregnant, some three years later, she suggested using the same name again if the baby was a girl. I had an instant negative reaction to that idea and I think I remember that David agreed with me. Anyway, the baby was my brother, Chuck, so it wasn't an issue. Two years later I finally got my sister, named Rochelle, and no mention of using the name Sarah again, which was fine with all of us. I'm sorry, though, that our Sarah is largely forgotten.

CHAPTER FIFTEEN

THE FIRST TIME I wrote an article for a newspaper I did not think of myself as a journalist. In fact, by most standards, I was not one, as I'd not studied the subject formally and didn't know much of newspaper jargon. I just thought of myself as a freelance writer who had landed an assignment with the Sunday magazine section of the *Chicago Tribune*. The assignment was to contribute to an ongoing feature at the back of the magazine, called First Person, which was written on alternating weeks by various freelance writers. One of those writers was moving to a public relations job – a conflict of interest for a newspaper writer – and they were looking for a replacement for her which, after my initial try-out, turned out to be me.

For First Person the writer interviewed someone about his or her job and then wrote the story as if the interviewee were telling it in her or his own words. This was pretty formulaic and after doing a few I could almost do them in my sleep. Still, it was a great way to learn about writing for a newspaper and, even more important, about interviewing.

In order to get my first chance I had to come up with a topic, several in fact for the editor to choose from, and arrange for the interview myself. I came up with about ten ideas and the editor, who over time I learned was a genius editor and a real tough cookie who knew how to test someone, picked the oddest of my suggestions. The minute I got the assignment I wished I'd never even thought of it.

My bright idea was to interview a toll booth collector. This is the person who sits in the little booth on a toll highway for eight hours at a time and takes people's money and gives them change when required and maybe says, "Drive safe now" or "Have a nice day." Or maybe says nothing or, worse yet, snarls. (These days there aren't many actual, live toll booth attendants since most lanes are automated in one way or another: you drop your coins into a machine – exact change required for this – or you get an account and pay electronically as you drive through.) Exactly what was I going to do with this assignment? What could a person with a job like that have to say that would fill up the entire back page of the Sunday magazine section?

The Toll Authority in Illinois, as it happens, is very picky about who they let talk to their employees. But I jumped through the hoops and eventually got approval for one hour in a little office with Janice Hope (not her real name), toll collector extraordinaire, and what a lucky break I had.

Collecting tolls on the highway, even in the middle of the night, even in the dead of winter when you can see your breath but you can't feel your fingertips, turns out to be like most anything else in life: exactly what you make of it. And Janice made plenty of it. She actually loved her job. She loved the races she'd have with the other toll collectors to see who could get the most cars through in a set time. She loved the dogs that stuck their heads out the windows and licked her hands. She loved her regulars, who came through at the same time every day and always came to her booth even if her line was longer.

And she loved getting involved in people's lives. Her favorite experience was when a man she knew came through her line and gave her a small package to give to the woman in the car behind him. She passed the package on and learned later it was an engagement ring. She had participated in the marriage proposal. But not all deliveries were so pleasant. Once she was called and asked to look for a certain car and then send the driver back to the hospital because his relative had died. "I found the man," she said, "asked him to pull over and called a state trooper to give him the news."

People sometimes gave her garbage to throw out for them. She didn't mind. Sometimes they'd pay her in pennies, even handing her the coins in a bag. She didn't mind that either, though she admitted she couldn't take the time to count the coins and had to trust that people were honest. Usually they were, she said. She couldn't recount how many times she'd reach out and close someone's gas tank for them.

Did anything annoy her? Well, she didn't like it when people asked her what the weather was like up north in Wisconsin or how the traffic was downtown. But she was always polite, she said, when she told them she didn't know. And she didn't like it when people would drive up to her window with the money in their mouths and pull it out and give it to her. She washed her hands on every break.

Janice was even a bit of a local celebrity. Since her booth was close to the Chicago suburb she lived in, people recognized her from the toll road if they saw her on the street or in the grocery store. She loved the attention. And she loved her job, said she'd hate to work in an office where she couldn't see the sunsets. Said she'd be bored to death at a desk and probably fall asleep for lack of fresh air.

My story was a hit. The editor liked it. The readers liked it. A textbook publisher liked it and paid me to let them use a couple paragraphs in a book on writing. A local radio personality liked it so much he interviewed Janice on his show. Boy, was I lucky. Yes, I did a good job writing it, but I might have bombed on my first flight if I'd gotten any of the toll collectors I usually run into on toll roads all over the country. They are not generally such a cheerful lot. So Janice deserves a fair amount of the credit for launching my journalism career.

A few months after the story appeared I went through her line just to say hello and see how she was liking her dance with celebrity. Of course she loved it. So much that she paid my toll for me. Forty cents. My first perk in my writing career. But don't tell the paper. It might not have been allowed; but then I never took that journalism ethics course, so how would I know?

Looking back at some of those early stories I see how the world has changed. When I interviewed what used to be known as an Avon Lady, a door-to-door Avon cosmetics salesperson, the most amazing thing about this woman's story, at that time, was that she told me that after she'd ring a bell she felt like running away before they could answer. My editor was also surprised by that and even put it into the headline. But now the most surprising thing is that she actually rang doorbells and went into strangers' homes. They weren't afraid to invite her in and she wasn't afraid to go in. They'd sometimes make a pot of coffee for her and tell her all about their lives and she'd spend as much as a couple hours with someone, unannounced and unexpected. It's hard to believe that the world has become such a different place – a place where you don't open your door for strangers and where door-to-door selling is largely a thing of the past – in just a little more than 30 years. But in this salesperson's territory, a neighborhood on the Southwest side of Chicago, in the early 1980s, most women were still stay-at-home moms who welcomed a diversion.

I thought a psychotherapist I interviewed would have the best stories and no doubt she did, but she couldn't share them with me. That wouldn't be legal. She believed that everyone is scared to death inside and putting up a good front. Or not so good, so they go to see her. She saw clients in the morning and at night, taking every afternoon off to do whatever she wanted because she did not see how she could lead anyone to a satisfying life if she didn't have a terrific life herself.

And then there was the power cleaner, a woman who cleaned people's houses after they had fires or floods or other huge disasters in their homes. She loved taking everything out of drawers and washing the inside of a dresser. Her only complaint was when people used spray wax. She said that gave the furniture a coating that she couldn't get under to really clean. Stuffed animals and shoes are hard to clean, too, it turns out. She learned to use her stemware and nice things every day, she said, because you never know what can happen. One day a torrent of mucky water might gush out of a pipe and into your cabinet and ruin your best dishes forever.

A courtroom illustrator whose story I told felt her profession was about to disappear as cameras came into the courtroom. She loved the excitement of the trials and told me of a couple riots that broke out and a case where someone brought a gun into the courtroom for the defendant, concealed in a book. This couldn't happen today with modern security. Her favorite trials were the ones with mobsters and loan sharks. She said they were the most colorful to draw. I'll bet they were nothing compared to today's courtroom characters. I hope she's spending her retirement sitting in some park in Chicago just sketching the kids with their tattoos and piercings. That sounds like the dream retirement for a courtroom illustrator. Or maybe she's still working – as it turns out, cameras have not made artists obsolete at trials yet.

To all these people, I listened and listened.

After a couple years of writing First Person stories I began to take assignments from other sections of the paper as well. I launched a monthly column for the travel section called Traveling With. It was really just a twist on the personality profiles I was becoming known for. Each month I would profile some celebrity who had a connection to travel. I wrote about how Itzhak Perlman traveled with his violin and how Rick Steves did his travel shows and wrote his books about Europe. I wrote about columnist Dave Barry and football coach John Madden and newsman Charles Kuralt and comic actor Michael Palin. Even the astronaut, Mae Jemison, who traveled on the space shuttle, Endeavor, in 1992, and said she would go anywhere, in or out of the world. It was all over the board, but everyone was ready to hit the road at any time, whether by bus or plane or train. Or even into space.

We decided to start with a splash: big name celebrity and odd-ball travel connection, in order to get attention for the column. I picked O.J. Simpson because everybody knew and loved him (Yes, loved. Do you remember those days?) and he did those commercials for Hertz Rent-A-Car where he ran through the airport. It was nine months before the Brentwood murders. We did the interview by phone. He was in a car (the Ford Bronco? I don't know; I had no reason to ask the make of the car at the time) driving his son to play at a friend's house. He was absolutely charming. I'm the last person in the United States to give up and admit he must have been guilty.

Here I was lucky again as I launched this new feature. O.J. told me what it was like to be O.J. in an airport. How he was always recognized and couldn't find a quiet corner to hide, even in the executive lounges. How he almost always rode first class because of his size. He talked about his grueling schedule of flying coast to coast to do color for football games and act in movies. When I recently reread the story I was shocked to learn that the words I live by and tell my children when they fly, "drink a lot of water and not much alcohol," were his.

The story ran in September, 1993 and his wife, Nicole, and her friend, Ron Goldman, were murdered in June, 1994. All hell broke loose. O.J. was front page news seemingly for ages, until the trial was finally over. The nation was riveted during the high-speed chase in his Bronco and everyone was speculating about whether he was attempting to get to the airport to escape. An article appeared in one of the major magazines – maybe *People*, I don't remember – quoting O.J. as saying, "I don't have the kind of face that can just sit on a chair at an airport and wait for the flight." Meaning even O.J. himself must have known he couldn't go undetected through an airport. That quote was taken from my article.

Actually, I was writing for the travel section for some time before I started the column. I wrote all the requisite beginner stories about romantic get-aways for Valentine's Day, where to go to see the leaves change color in autumn, and an assortment of bed-and-breakfast pieces about owners who had unusual reasons for wanting to run an inn. My favorite early piece for the section was an article called "The First Time I Saw Paris" in which I interviewed people who had a long-time association with Paris, and asked them to talk about their first encounters with the famed city.

I included in that story Pierre Salinger of the Kennedy administration, chef Julia Child, the artist and celebrity caricaturist Al Hirschfeld, columnist Art Buchwald, and Hollywood personality Eva Gabor, all, sadly, no longer on this earth. Everyone was generous with their memories and claimed never to have been asked about their first impressions of Paris. Art Buchwald and Al

Hirschfeld went there in the 1920's and were swept away by the heady arts and literary atmosphere. Eva Gabor was brought there by her parents when she was 14 and on her first night made a pig of herself, she said, on delicious raspberries and heavy cream. Salinger's first trip as an adult (he went as a babe in arms, but had no memory of the occasion) was to set up a press conference for President Kennedy for whom he was working as press secretary at the time. Julia Child went as a young bride. Within a month she was studying at the Cordon Bleu, and has been associated with French cooking forever since.

There are all kinds of ways to be a travel writer. I did most of my writing from the comfort of my own desk. I called people to get information or do telephone interviews, but didn't necessarily visit the place I was writing about. Once in a while I went on a trip, but most of the time it was all in my head or in the heads of the people I interviewed. My best actual trip was to the Lightning Field in west central New Mexico. In truth, it was a bit of a nightmare, but it made a great story. The Lightning Field is an artistic installation in one of the loneliest areas of the state. There are 400 steel rods, honed to a point at the top, stuck in the ground. You view them over a 24-hour period, experiencing them in every different possible light. If it rains and there's lightning, so much the better, but it isn't necessary for full enjoyment of the exhibit.

The visitor must spend the night in a small cabin at the edge of the field. The cabin holds six in very tight quarters but I was there with my husband and no one else. You are picked up in the town of

Quemado, where you are told to wait for your ride at the two-story building. There is only one main street and only one two-story building in town. From there you are driven out to the cabin, about a half hour ride, as I recall, then shown where the food is, how to lock the door, and how to call for help on a short-wave radio. Then you are left in this cabin in the wilderness with the 400 poles outside for 24 hours. You have to trust that someone will come back for you.

We were picked up by a woman and her eight-year-old daughter. As soon as we settled into their Jeep the little girl said to her mother, "Did you tell them about the snakes?" It followed along in the same vein for the rest of the trip. We were warned about all sorts of critters and, indeed, after an uneasy night, found a variety of animal excrement in corners of the cabin the next day. I won't say it was fun, but it was definitely not your usual weekend retreat. I recommend it, if you don't mind not being sure you'll ever get home.

We had this little adventure shortly after we moved to New Mexico, so we weren't really used to how strange this state can be. When I first moved here from Chicago I had several assignments from the paper, and continued to write for them for a few years. My editor at the travel section told me when I left, sure, keep writing for us. But don't ever send me anything about Santa Fe. Seen it all. Introduce Chicagoans to something different. Hence, the Lightning Field. It was the most different thing I ever came up with.

Travel writing is thought of as a most glamorous field. It might be if you work for one of the slick magazines. Or for a small, local paper where your ethics aren't likely to be questioned. But major newspapers don't allow reporters to write about anything where the subject has paid the writer in any way, including any expenses incurred. Once in a while the paper would pay, but usually it was up to me to cover the travel costs. I tried to bundle stories with trips I was already taking. So I'd go visit my sister in D.C., let's say, and line up two or three interviews there. I would get people with a story to tell, but never hot enough for the paper to pay someone just to go out there to do the interview. This, as I've said, is also how I got the Nu Shu story in Taiwan.

SINCE I'D ALWAYS WANTED to write in some form, it follows that I was interested in other writers. Once I started writing for the *Tribune* I tried to be the one assigned to interview authors whenever possible. And once I started down that road, I began to get books from publishers until eventually I was looking for ways to get rid of them in order to make room for me to sit at my desk.

While the guy-next-door interviews were the most fun, the celebrities, and especially the writers, were each compelling in their own way. Some were celebrities who had just written a book about their lives. They weren't actual writers, of course – sometimes the books were even ghost-written – but I loved meeting them. Like

Debbie Reynolds and Lauren Bacall. Bacall – she was Betty to her friends but I didn't dare call her that – was the most intimidating. We had breakfast together at the Four Seasons hotel in Chicago and she ordered a plate of bacon and ate it all. I ordered a bagel, which came with two bagels on the plate, and agonized through the whole meal as to whether I should offer her one. Finally, she said she was on a no-carb diet, so I know she wouldn't have taken one, but I still wonder if I should have offered.

I have never met such a cool customer in my life. She knew exactly who she was. It seemed nothing could intimidate her. Well, I guess having been married to her adored Bogie and palling around with the likes of Adlai Stevenson and Leonard Bernstein and Hepburn and Tracy helped her develop a bit of self-confidence.

Then there were the real writers: Mary Gordon, Amy Tan, Marianne Wiggins, to name a few. Wiggins I hadn't heard of before the interview but discovered that she'd been married to Salmon Rushdie during the time of the Fatwa. In fact, her book, *John Dollar*, was released at the same time as Rushdie's *Satanic Verses*. She couldn't do any promotional work for her own book because she had to go into hiding with Rushdie. She said that "living on the lam" was just "another accommodation of the type that women have to make all the time." She was not resentful, but was separated from Rushdie at the time of the interview in 1991, in part, she said, because he had become more religious, and she said she would never turn to God. "I'm opinionated as hell," she said, "and I shoot my mouth off and nobody can stop me." I thought she was terrific.

(Years later I read *Joseph Anton*, Rushdie's memoir of his years in hiding, and got a different view of their relationship.)

I think now that the independent professional women I interviewed had a huge effect on me. I was raised to serve; the expectation was that I would be a wife and mother. Period. I don't blame my parents. It's the way things were when I was a child. I had to relearn my entire view of life after I had three children, had returned to school and then become a newspaper writer. I came to realize that not all women who worked were just doing it because they had to, which had been my only motivation in the beginning. At some point in the seventies one of my young children asked – in a family group that included my mother – "Who is Gloria Steinem?" My mother immediately answered, "She's a bad lady." I was flabbergasted but, also, my whole life fell into place at that moment. I realized the indoctrination I had received and the messages I had internalized.

But I knew what I had to do, for the sake of my children if for no other reason, so they did not get led down the same path of thinking a woman's place is only in the home. That she shouldn't work if her salary was not needed. I started by getting my mother to amend her answer, which she did, grudgingly. She wouldn't go so far as to say Steinem wasn't bad, but she did sign off on the notion that she had done some interesting things that had made her famous. Small victory, but worth the effort, I thought, so at least the kids would not come away with the impression that I agreed with my mother's initial assessment.

I had become sort of my own therapist, with the help of all the strong women I met and one or two real therapists, and I never looked back. The author, Bharati Mukherjee, told me something about life that I should have known but did not realize until I met her. She reminded me that in India one cannot change one's status or reinvent oneself as we can in the West. Her name, she said, announces to anyone who knows the Bengali language, both the region of India she comes from and her caste. She is from Calcutta, and is a member of the elite Brahmin class. When she is in India, that is who she is.

She grew up in a home with a large extended family where, as she put it, "Closing a door or wanting space for yourself was considered a selfish act." She went to college in America and married the American writer, Clark Blaise. She holds a double doctorate in English and comparative literature from the University of Iowa and three master's degrees (in English and in ancient Indian culture from the University of Baroda in India, and a Master of Fine Arts from the University of Iowa).

For a long time I'd been intensely aware of the difficulty of being the sort of ethnic minority who can be identified by the color of her skin or certain features of her appearance. But to be limited by one's name? To be assigned a caste? I had never thought of this. With all the obstacles put on people, especially women, both historically and today, this is just another particularly onerous one. Mukherjee decided she could not live with the limitations India put on women. Despite her education and other accomplishments, if she had returned to India to live she would have had to marry a man of her father's choosing. She decided to remain in the West.

But most people live with self-imposed limitations, men and women alike. We tell ourselves we can't do this or that. We might live our whole lives repeating negative messages we received as children, often from our parents. These can be more difficult to escape than cultural rules that might be evaded just by moving from East to West. We must do a lot more work than that to erase some of those messages, and sometimes we don't succeed no matter what we do. Sometimes we are like the insects – fruit flies I think they were – in the famous experiment where the scientist took the lid off the jar in which they were flying around and they still didn't fly up any higher than the top of the glass. Like those insects we sometimes get trapped in a prison that isn't even locked, a prison of our own making. I am thankful to Marianne Wiggins and Lauren Bacall and so many others who crossed my path and allowed me a brief glimpse into their lives. They helped me to expand my own view of life.

CHAPTER SIXTEEN

"Not every story is a winner." An editor said that to me once. It was not good news. The particular story he made that comment about was not a disaster. We fixed it and it ran.

But sometimes a story is "killed." The newspaper or magazine does not run it. It could be the fault of the writer, or of the subject of the story. It might be the fault of the editor. It's possible it was nobody's fault; circumstances just made it impossible to print the article. Depending on the particular situation, if the article doesn't run, the writer should get a "kill fee" – full or partial payment, based on the terms of the contract.

No one is happy when this happens. I've had a few situations where the idea just didn't pan out. The editor and I both thought it would work but it didn't. In one case, I was working on a story on non-traditional medicine when the editorial staff of the publication changed and the new editor was not interested in the subject. But he didn't tell me that. He just kept putting road blocks in the way of my completion of the research. "Check on this," "Talk to them," "Try this." It went on and on. Since I didn't know this person before, and had never encountered such a situation, it took me a while to figure out that he didn't want to run the story and didn't want to say so. Probably he wanted me to be the one to quit the project so it wouldn't be his responsibility. And that's what I did, finally. It just wasn't worth the trouble.

In another instance, I pitched a story idea to a small regional magazine in the Chicago area. It was about older adults returning to college to complete degree programs they had abandoned when they were younger. This was at a time when adults going to college was a new trend, a novel idea. The editor was enthusiastic. I wrote the story and submitted it. A fair amount of time went by but I heard nothing. No feedback and the article did not appear. Then, surprise, the magazine ran an article *very* similar to mine by another writer. I called and talked to the editor. She assured me this article was in the pipeline when I submitted my proposal. Then why did they accept mine? It was written by an intern, she said. That was a piece of information she never should have given me. It made everything clear. They assigned my idea to someone who would write it while on salary, or maybe even for free if she was an unpaid intern. Did they think I would never find out? I don't know. I can't remember if I got a kill fee. I hope so – I certainly should have. The best part of this tale is that the conversation ended with the editor saying, "Please let us know if you have any other ideas." Yeah, right.

Another time a story of mine was slated to run in the woman's section of a local newspaper. It was done, accepted, I'd even been paid in full, when a woman won the office of governor for the first time in the history of that state. The section decided to run a big story about her instead of my article and pushed mine down the line a few months. I had no problem with that. It was a perfectly logical and sensible decision. But in the interim, before the new date arrived, the newspaper changed the focus of the woman's section. No longer was it to contain serious articles. It became a forum for fashion news and the like. That was a decision I did *not* agree with. Not just because it meant my story would never run, but also because I felt it was a step backwards for the paper. Why were they going back to offering women stories about beauty salons at a time when women were finally being taken more seriously?

I never knew the answer to that. But I'm happy to take a few words here to tell the story that never got into print. It was about how women should be careful when selecting a lawyer to represent them in legal matters. My thesis was that while most lawyers are honest, as in any profession there are those who would take advantage of the vulnerable. I used divorce as an example of a time when a woman would be in an unfamiliar and emotional situation. She would naturally assume that her lawyer had her best interests at heart. And maybe the lawyer was wanting to achieve the best outcome for her client. But at the same time, some might also want to earn as much money as possible from the case.

This is a touchy subject. I interviewed several divorce lawyers. I talked with a number of psychologists who worked with women going through divorce. Many of the women they worked with had never had any dealings with a lawyer before, except maybe to write a will. And, of course, I spoke with women who had recently gone through the divorce process. I wrote the story. It was vetted and accepted so I think I represented all sides of the issue fairly.

As often happens in journalism, a story idea comes from life experience. And so it was with this one. After 44 years of marriage I was getting a divorce. I was stunned. I just wanted it over with. I hired a female lawyer thinking that because of her gender she would be understanding. That was naive and ridiculous. She also had a good reputation as near as I could tell. But a strange thing kept happening. No matter what I said I wanted, she said we couldn't ask for that. "His lawyer will never allow him to do that," she kept saying. At last I signed the papers. I set my pen down when I was finished. I looked up at her. "Is there anything else you want?" she asked. "Because we can go after him in court for more." Of course we could. That was the game all along. Start the cash register rolling again. I said, "No, thank you" and left.

I was very fortunate because mine was an amicable divorce. Everything I wanted but wasn't allowed to ask for had been promised to me by my husband before we even went to lawyers. He honored his promises and I knew he would. From what I heard researching the story, and from what I've heard since, I was one of the lucky ones.

I've included this story here because I think it's one that should be told. I'm happy to have the chance I didn't have before to warn people to be cautious in hiring a lawyer. But also I'm glad to be able to release a story into the world. What happens to the stories we don't tell? I've asked that question frequently as I've worked on this memoir. Sometimes you don't know what the stories have been doing to you until you let them out. I didn't include this story in the article I wrote. I never mentioned the name of the lawyer and won't do so here. That doesn't have to be known. People who are aware I've been through a divorce often ask me to recommend a lawyer. I always say, "I can only tell you who *not* to go to." And then I tell the name. I hope that's a fair compromise. Since she did not do any real damage to me (and since I'm scared to death of her and never want to see her again), I decided not to go public with allegations against her. I hope this is not too wimpy a response. I can only be what I am.

And one more thing: My body of work so far is largely non-fiction. But I have tried to write fiction at various times. My first accomplishment in that arena was *Lonely River Village*, a novel based on the translations of Nu Shu that I acquired. That was my first success and it won some awards. It was not my first attempt. There is the partially written, unpublished, mystery novel. I wrote the beginning and knew what the ending was going to be but couldn't figure out how to get there. An acquaintance who writes mysteries advised me to write the ending and said it would all fall into place. I wrote the ending. It didn't fall into place. The book is still sitting in a drawer. I can come back to it some day.

And there is the book – also unpublished – about a road trip – a classic topic. I know where it's going to end up but the protagonist is currently stranded on the way to her destination. I hope to help her complete the trip eventually but right now she's resting in a drawer too.

A couple other novels are waiting to be finished too. I'm hopeful about them, also.

I've spilled all this to complete the picture. I think sometimes we don't want to tell certain stories. But maybe some stories just don't want to be told. It's hard to know – when you hit that wall – what really is the problem. Truth be told, it could be lack of talent. I tell my writing workshop students that is not the case. Your stories are alive and you just have to find out how they want to be told. I tell myself that, too. I hope it's true.

CHAPTER SEVENTEEN

IF I HAD GIVEN NAMES to my chapters, I would have called this one "I Try to Write a Children's Book."

My attempt to do this resulted from the fact that there was one story I really wanted to tell but had struggled for decades to find a way to do it. It was a story I first heard as a child, maybe when I was around eight or nine years old. My first try at getting it on paper was at least thirty years ago, maybe more. I wrote it as a sort of essay, or framed story. I described how I used to watch my grandmother cook in her kitchen, and then recounted how she told me, on one cozy afternoon of dinner preparation, about how she learned to read. Born at the end of the nineteenth century, she grew up in what is now Belarus, the oldest of seven children, three boys and four girls. At that time the girls in her village – I'm not sure how widespread this was beyond the village as I never thought to ask – were not allowed to attend school. My grandmother learned to read by sneaking out of the house after the boys had gone and watching through the window of the school. I thought then, and I still think now, that that was a remarkable accomplishment.

I never tried to publish this essay, nor did I even have any idea where a story like this could be placed. Then, sometime around 1995, I submitted the essay to a writers' workshop and not only secured admission, but won a scholarship as well. I was elated. My essay must be really good, I thought.

But the joy did not last long. The workshop participants and the leader, an experienced, well-published essayist, tore my story to pieces. In a private tutorial session, the leader told me that the grandmother's voice was stilted. I said, "That's exactly how she talked." He said it didn't matter how she really sounded, that it just didn't read well. "Do you want to imitate your grandmother's speech patterns?" he asked me, "Or sell a story?"

I don't remember what I answered, but I know I was crushed. I wanted to represent my grandmother honestly. I thought – and still do – that her story was amazing. Learning to read by looking through the window of a school? Come on. That's amazing.

Over the ensuing years I tried different ways to write it. But I could never get her voice out of my head. It always came out sounding like her and that, I believed, was the problem. I had been told so by an expert.

Then a few years ago it occurred to me to write the story as a children's book. That released me somehow. Now my grandmother was no longer telling her story to me; a little girl was the center of the action. I wrote it pretty quickly. I put my grandmother's entire family into it and imagined the reaction they would have to her learning to read in this way. I liked it. A few friends read it in this form and liked it. I was ready to go.

Except for one thing: a children's book needs illustrations. I can't draw, so an illustrator would have to be found. Illustrated

books are expensive to publish. It's hard to find a publisher for anything in these times, let alone a picture book, precisely because it's
expensive to get the drawings. I spoke to some artist friends and
they weren't encouraging. They told me that if I wanted to publish
myself I would have to buy all the pictures in advance from an
artist. This was much too big an investment for me so I shelved the
idea again.

Then I met a writer who had very successfully published a book
as a joint effort with an illustrator, the two of them agreeing to
share the profits, whatever they might be. I met the artist and asked
if she would be willing to enter into such an arrangement with me.
She read the manuscript and declined. Rejected again.

I have to say that writing a book that needs illustrations just
opens up more ways that a writer can be rejected. At least that's
how I felt as I put the book away again for a few more years.

Until I happened upon an artist who liked the story and was
willing to take a chance. There are no guarantees, I told her, especially publishing it ourselves. Dear person that she is, she said, "I
love to draw, so why not?" We worked on the book for about eight
months and she created some very clever drawings for the story.
Hannah's Day at School was born. It is recently published and
doing very well so far. When I hold it in my hands I am satisfied
that I honored my grandmother and wrote a book that encourages
girls to fight for an education, if fighting is necessary in the culture
in which they live.

CHAPTER EIGHTEEN

ALL THE TIME I was writing I was also teaching. My teaching career had started back in 1964 when I was 21 years old. I was sent, like all rookie teachers in the Chicago Public Schools system in those days, to one of the toughest schools in one of the most troubled neighborhoods: Schiller Elementary, in the middle of the Cabrini-Green housing projects. The area was sometimes referred to as the inner city, sometimes Cabrini-Green, sometimes just the projects. Use any of those terms to describe where you were teaching and people turned pale, shrieked or gasped. It had a reputation.

Well-earned, too. I was given a class of 48 third graders who ranged in age from eight – the age they were supposed to be – to eleven. There were no assistants or teachers' aids. I'd never even heard the term teacher's aid in those days.

Forty-eight kids – some could read, some couldn't. Some could add and subtract, some could barely count. It was exactly the nightmare you would imagine it to be. Every Sunday night for two years – except during summer vacations – I cried. I flung myself across my brand-new queen size marriage bed and sobbed because I could not imagine how I was going to get up the next morning and go back to that hell. The system was just senseless. And positively brutal. The longer you taught the more you worked your way up into better neighborhoods. Which left the least experienced – or those with no experience at all – in the schools that needed savvy teachers the most.

Forty-eight students was the maximum number allowed in a classroom in Illinois in those days and that's what we got. Most of these kids were doomed to failure by the time I met them. I had no training for dealing with the particular issues of this community. I had thought this third grade was going to be just like my own third grade class when I was a child – children reasonably well-behaved, teachers competent and in control – which I could still remember vividly since I was not that far past it. I tried my best. But I didn't know what to do. I think I really helped a few of them. I know I was completely useless to the others.

I hated failing. I hated finding out about this neighborhood – in the same city where I grew up, a city I loved – where people shot guns out of windows, toddlers were raped in elevators, siblings shared snow boots in the winter and attended school only when it was their turn for the boots, and a mother punched her son in the nose in front of the teacher – me – to show she was sincerely trying to raise her child right.

After two years I got pregnant and quit. I had wanted to teach, not babysit, and that was still what I wanted. But after having three children in three and a half years I knew that even in the best teaching situation it was either going to be *my* kids or the *other* kids. No way was I going to be able to spend a day with a classroom full of children and then come home to my own children and be a good mother. Lots of women do it but I knew I couldn't.

I was still trying to write but not making any money at it yet and I knew I had to do something. I had a Bachelor's Degree in education and decided to go back to school, part time, for a Master's Degree in literature. (Since I was such a heavy-duty reader that seemed like a natural choice, and it was.) I took four years to complete, as a part-time student, what would have otherwise been a two-year program, and there was lots of maneuvering with baby sitters. I eventually settled into a routine of exchanging child care with other mothers who had returned to school. This, of course, meant that during much of my at-home time I had a house full of kids, but somehow it all worked out. I also had a little help from my own mother, who frowned on the whole enterprise but helped anyway. When I completed the program I returned to teaching as a writing and literature instructor at a community college, which I loved. And just as I settled into that, I began to earn money as a writer. And I loved that, too. I kept on doing both.

Between the two jobs, each not quite full time but more than half time, and taking care of three kids with my husband frequently out of the country on business, I was pretty exhausted most of the time. I tried to do all my writing while the kids were at school. I did most of my teaching in the evening, which I preferred because I had more adult students. In the morning I got the kids off to school and when they came home I packed up my work.

Despite the misguided advice of my mother that I shouldn't be working at all because it would not be good for my marriage, I prided myself that the kids almost didn't know I worked at all. After school it was often our house where the neighborhood kids hung out because their mothers were playing tennis or whatever. In fact the neighbors barely knew I worked, either. Even though a minimum of one article per week appeared under my byline, frequently more, everyone, including my own mother, seemed unaware of my "other" job. The teaching they understood. But anything done at home was not considered work.

As I look back, I think I was pretty ambivalent about the whole thing. My own husband, in fact, was not much impressed, frequently hinting that I should get a "full time" job by saying things like, all the women he knew at work were on a "different track." Meaning they had real careers and were making better money than I was. I did try it for a year, with a job writing for the dairy industry. It was maddening. The pace was so slow I used to sit at my computer dreaming of the laundry I could be doing if I were home. When you are used to working on your own time and juggling everything successfully or falling on your face, you learn to work fast. After about a year on that job my boss called me into her office and told me I had to slow down and stop finishing projects so fast. I quit instead, and went back to writing, teaching, cooking, cleaning, and doing laundry at breakneck speed. I'd been spoiled forever by being my own boss for so long.

After living this way for decades, now it goes almost without saying that I can't slow down. I dream of a relaxed retirement (or at least semi-retirement) and it goes from dream to nightmare. I've had a few times in my life when my work stalled and I was teetering at the edge of depression because I felt guilty for not doing enough. I was afraid that if I stopped I'd feel lost again. I seemed to believe that I could only enjoy leisure if I had worked myself to death and was exhausted. Then I'd earned a rest and could take it easy for a few days without feeling guilty. Some of this may have come from the feeling of always needing to prove that what I was doing was worthwhile and deserving of respect. I think I bounced back and forth from my childhood indoctrination that I should only be a wife and mother, and the rest of the world telling me that I should be working. My choice was to be working, but it's hard to get those old messages out of your head.

One good thing came out of all this: my innovation called "reading week." That was the week between Christmas and New Year's, a time when school is out and lots of people aren't working so you can't make any headway pitching stories or trying to set up interviews. I let myself do nothing but read. And allowed myself to not feel guilty about it. I still stay to this schedule even though I'm not pitching stories or teaching anymore. With the kids all grown and out of the house it's even easier. I don't deny myself a holiday party or daily walk, but what would normally be work time is reading time. It's very therapeutic and, for a lover of books, a wonderful way to spend a week.

CHAPTER NINETEEN

WHILE TEACHING OR RESEARCHING my three big stories, I continued to do interviews and write articles for the *Chicago Tribune*. One of my favorites was the actor Clayton Moore, who played the Lone Ranger on television. I interviewed him by phone from my home office. He was in his apartment in Los Angeles. The interview was arranged with the help of his daughter, who showed enormous concern for him and suggested that he hadn't had much attention lately and would be happy to speak with me for an hour or so.

He sounded strained, almost weak. There were lots of directions I would have loved to go with the interview, but I was restricted by the space limits of the column. This story was for the Chicago Voices feature I mentioned earlier, where well-known people who lived or used to live in Chicago talked about their lives in the city when they were growing up, and basically always said how wonderful Chicago was and what a positive contribution the city had made to their lives. It was only about 800 words long and once you got all the required stuff in you had just about filled your quota. The column only lasted a couple years because how long could people keep reading about how great Chicago was? It was hugely popular, though, because everybody wanted to see who would be the surprise Chicagoan each week.

During our conversation Moore made some remarks about something he wished he could do; I can't remember exactly what it was anymore. I answered, really meaning it as a joke, by saying that of course he could do this since he was the Lone Ranger. There was a pause. "I'm not the Lone Ranger," he said with an air of profound sadness. "I'm an actor. Or was."

This part of the interview did not find its way into the story. There was no place for it. It didn't fit the parameters. I was able to write about the fact that he wanted to be a cowboy when he grew up. Not an actor. And I included all the stuff he did growing up in Chicago, especially that he started his show business career in a flying trapeze act. He went to the same high school I did, but I couldn't include that. This type of writing was frustrating because it was so limited. But it was easy and fun because I had mastered the formula. The first time I wrote this type of article for the *Chicago Tribune* it took me two weeks from interview to finished product. By the end of my tenure with them I could do the same thing in closer to two hours. Computers helped of course – I was using a typewriter when I first started – but the real thing was that I understood how to write to the formula. But was that writing?

Yes, I think it was. For me, anyway. I learned how to write on the job. How to write fast. How to listen. How to be accurate. And I enlarged my world view, which was going to prepare me for later when I was ready to put the Nu Shu story into book form. And, eventually, with perseverance, the Crypto-Jewish story. Maybe even the story of the women pioneer diaries. Writing book-length was a skill I didn't have yet, and a skill not easily acquired. Along the way, I met and wrote about hundreds of people, all with stories to tell. Most of the stories found their way into the *Chicago Tribune*, some into other smaller – but fun to write for – publications. Local newspapers and newsletters, for the most part. Even a few for the *Albuquerque Journal* after I moved to New Mexico.

Two writers who had a huge influence on me were older women – now both deceased. They broke the mold in terms of what women could do in the world in general, and in writing in particular. Their names might not be easily recognized, but their accomplishments were huge: Ethel Payne and Emily Hahn.

Ethel Payne was the granddaughter of a slave and one of the first African American journalists to be accredited to the White House Press Corps. She had made the news herself when she asked President Eisenhower a question about segregation and the next day the *Washington Star* carried the headline: "Negro Woman Reporter Angers Ike."

She told me how hard she had to work to get an education, sandwiching college classes between jobs. She wanted to be a lawyer but came up against discrimination both because she was a woman and because she was African American. Her mother encouraged her to write, and that's how she finally found her way to journalism. I interviewed her in her apartment in Washington, D.C. in 1988. It was one of those stories I got because I happened to be traveling that way. I was nervous because I was so in awe of what she had accomplished. And, she had invited me for lunch, which was a far more gracious offer than I'd ever had from anyone I was interviewing. I declined her invitation to share a bottle of wine because alcohol makes me sleepy and I knew from the first minute that I would need all my faculties to keep up with her intellectually. She was frankly disappointed – "oh, poo," she said – but she was charming and delightful and we got along famously after that was settled. She served tuna salad if I remember correctly.

Emily Hahn had quite a different story. She was an adventurous young woman who traveled all over the world, starting with a United States cross-country driving trip in a Model-T Ford in 1924 at the age of 19. She wrote letters home describing her adventures and her brother-in-law sent some to *The New Yorker* magazine. They published them. When I met her in 1989 it was in her office at *The New Yorker*. And, truth be told, when my editor suggested I interview her because I was going to New York anyway, I didn't really know anything about her. But I grabbed at the chance because I wanted to see what *The New Yorker* offices looked like – I'd been reading that magazine since I was a kid. All the way back to a time when all I cared about were the cartoons.

What a lucky break for me. It turned out she had grown up in Chicago, so we had that in common from the start. She'd written 56 books and had managed to be in places like China and Africa when the most exciting things were happening. And all because a college adviser had discouraged her from pursuing a degree in engineering, telling her "the female mind is incapable of grasping mechanics or higher mathematics." This infuriated her, of course. She did join the Geology Club in college even though the sign for meetings said "Women Not Invited" at the bottom. "I just went and eventually they accepted me," she said.

She was a Harvey Girl (working for the Fred Harvey restaurants associated with the railroad) for a while in New Mexico, leading tours around the state. She became an opium user while she was living in China. I asked her how she quit the opium and she said, "I just stopped." Our interview ended with a big hug; it was a special treat to see *The New Yorker* offices, but nothing compared to meeting this woman. Some years before she died she moved to England and we exchanged a few letters. She was alert and interested in the world to the very end – as I would have expected.

CHAPTER TWENTY

ONE OF THE ELEMENTS that drew me into the Converso story was the importance of family. Most Conversos that I met were more concerned about how talking publicly about their Jewish heritage would affect their families than they were about any danger connected with their Jewish history. I understood that, especially as I contemplated writing my memoir. I, too, worried about divulging something about our family that others would find objectionable.

My siblings and I formed a rather unusual group, two small, separate families, really. I was the oldest, then there was David and Alan. Then came the lost baby, Sarah. After a break of several years, Chuck and Rochelle joined the clan, a little family unto themselves. I was twelve when Chuck was born and almost fifteen when Rochelle came along. I have some memories of their childhood, but no memories of playing with them in the way David and Alan and I played together.

My mother, who was reasonably attentive to her first three children, was a little vague when these last two came along. I don't know how to describe it; maybe I shouldn't say anything. I was a teenager, after all, and busy becoming whoever I was going to become. There were a few boyfriends here and there. I wasn't involved in the day-to-day lives of these two cute little kids. I do remember once when Chuck tumbled down a few stairs – he must have been around two years old – and my mother, pregnant with Rochelle, responded to my announcement that he had fallen and was crying with "Give him a rattle."

That must have been the best she could do at that moment. She certainly let my friends and me feed the little ones whenever we wanted to. And sometimes we enjoyed playing mommy and helping her out. She was tired by then. She was a woman with a driver's license and no car to drive. And no place to go. And now five children to take care of.

When a Converso would tell me they were researching their history but didn't want their family to know, or the family all knew they were Crypto-Jews but didn't want anyone to talk about it, I understood. I would never knowingly tell something about my siblings that they didn't want announced to the world. But in the case of these people who were living a double life there was a real pull in two directions that they had to fight: how to be true to themselves and at peace with those they loved who saw the world in other ways. To say they were often conflicted would be putting it very mildly.

In the course of interviewing dozens of Conversos, most in New Mexico, a few in Texas and California, I met one woman in particular who touched my heart. I prefer not to use her real name because, although she is now deceased, many of her relatives still live in New Mexico and they prefer privacy. And I want to respect that. So I will call her Rebecca.

It was with great satisfaction and much excitement that I reached into my collection of taped interviews a couple years ago and found the two tapes of my interviews with Rebecca. They were almost twenty years old by then. I kept them for the same reason I kept tapes of all my interviews: just in case. Luckily my old-fashioned tape player still worked. Not so lucky, the tapes were dried from almost two decades in arid New Mexico. I could play them, and I could hear Rebecca's voice, but I couldn't understand everything she was saying. So far I haven't found anyone who can find the technology to bring her voice back to me as it was when I first met her. I don't actually need it because I also have notes, but I'd really love to hear her again as she sounded when I knew her.

Rebecca was university educated, both in the sciences and the arts. She was a genuine Crypto-Jew who knew from childhood that she was Jewish, and who practiced Judaism in secret while outwardly observing the Catholic faith. She was one of several Conversos who told me that their families possessed the key to their ancestral homes in Toledo, Spain. The first time I heard this from someone I was amazed. I wondered not only how they were able to keep the key in the family – and know what it was for – over more than five hundred years, but why they took it in the first place. It was a while before I realized that the people who left Spain at the time of the Expulsion had no idea if they would ever return. Many of them would have thought that at some point they or their descendants might return. For all they knew, the whole thing might have blown over in twenty years. Maybe a new king would come to power. As it happened, even new rulers didn't change anything and the Office of the Inquisition continued its work for centuries.

One thing Rebecca told me that no one else ever has, is something I really couldn't believe when she first said it. She insisted that when she would walk down a street in Albuquerque and pass a person of Spanish descent she could tell by looking at him or her whether they were descended from Jews or from Inquisitors. When she told me that, more than twenty years ago, it seemed impossible. Now, though I would not claim the same skill, I have come to a point where I can get a sense of it when I get to know someone. Of course, I never ask. But frequently, when someone I meet knows of my research, they will bring their family stories – or just their suspicions – to me.

I should mention here that the governments of Spain and Portugal are now giving a path to citizenship for descendants of those expelled during the Inquisition. There are plenty of hoops for these people to jump through, but many are choosing to do it. Remember, in today's world Spanish citizenship confers European Union citizenship as well. But several Conversos have told me that they feel a genuine pull toward Spain, often because a grandparent or some other relative instilled a love of the country in them, despite the ugly history.

Rebecca told me many things about life as a secret Jew. How the family covered the mirrors in their home when mourning a death, a Jewish practice. How they washed a baby thoroughly after his baptism to get all the holy water off of him. How they kept a pig as a pet, sold it when it was fully grown, but never butchered it or ate pork. They felt having a pet pig would make them look absolutely not Jewish, because it is forbidden for Jews to eat pork. Every one of these behaviors, and many more, were told to me over and over by different individuals and families.

Rebecca was among a growing group of Conversos who opted to return to open Jewish practice. Most do not, but those who do, prefer the word "return" over "convert" to describe the process of becoming fully Jewish. They feel their ancestors were forced to leave Judaism and if that hadn't happened they would still be Jewish so there is no need for them to convert. They do study and fill in all the blanks in their Jewish education. They correct the misperceptions that have resulted from centuries of practice without the guidance of rabbis or Torah. And then they return.

CHAPTER TWENTY-ONE

I THINK WHAT ASTOUNDED ME the most when I started reading the journals and letters of American pioneer women was when someone would write that she baked a pie for dinner. And that, following walking fourteen miles during the day while carrying her small child. And then noted, in passing, that she was expecting another little one soon (no one ever seemed to use the word "pregnant.") There were many versions of this report: a child was lost and had to be found; grandma was depressed and had spent many days on the bed or mattress in the steamy, hot wagon; one of the family's wagons broke down and many family treasures had to be discarded on the trail to make room for food and other necessities to be jammed into another wagon. (Some entrepreneurial types made a business of traveling behind wagon trains and picking up discarded items to sell.) The list goes on. Essentially, the men planned the route and drove the wagons and the women managed just about everything else. And when the day was over many of these women wrote in their journals. They recorded the number of graves the wagon train passed that day. They told of their experiences on the trail, their fears, their joys. They told how many miles they had traveled and what they prepared for each meal that day. They walked almost the whole way. The wagons were for chickens, baby animals that couldn't manage the walk yet, or for the sick and elderly. (Many a grandma came along for the ride, knowing she might not survive the trip but not wanting to be left back home without family.) Sometimes the elderly wrote. Sometimes the daughter or daughter-in-law care-taker wrote. After she finished her chores.

That's why I don't have a lot of sympathy for people who tell me they have a book in them but don't have time to write. Or for myself when I feel too busy or tired to write. I know from these women that if the will is there, it can be done.

Something very important to remember about these women is that most of them were not on the trail because they wanted to be. They were there because a father or husband decided to make the journey west and they had to go along. (Very few single women went on their own. Those who did were often nurses or teachers.) Still, they did what was required of them. And then they wrote. Sometimes a husband died along the way and his wife took over driving the wagon. She would stake out a homestead for herself and her children when they reached the end of the trail. And then she wrote the story.

Not to pick a quarrel with the likes of Lewis and Clark and other explorers – they wrote fine journals – but if you want to know how families traveled west you need to read the women's diaries. In recent years more of these have come to light. Some are highly edited or written by educated women. Many are unedited, pretty raw, lacking correct spelling and punctuation because the women who wrote them were not formally educated. But they wrote. And because of them we know so much more about what really happened on the trail.

My personal connection to these women writers was even slimmer than my connection to the Nu Shu writers. And far less than with the many people I interviewed for newspaper articles or Converso research. Just when I thought that this would always be an academic enterprise, I remembered that I knew of a modern-day pioneer of sorts who wrote a journal about her adventures. I didn't know her personally, but I knew her relatives. And, in fact, she had only passed away about a year before I encountered her journal. And, with full disclosure, I must tell you that her relatives are my relatives: she is the great aunt of my daughter-in-law.

Ethyle Town was not a pioneer in the sense that she traveled west in a covered wagon. But her family had come to America from Britain and settled in Maryland. Then they moved farther west and became Illinois farmers. She continued their adventurous tradition by serving in the Navy and traveling the world. The portion of her diary that I was able to read describes a trip to Africa and a week spent with Albert Schweitzer and his team of medical personnel in 1957.

Her journey began on a plane, a Pan Am Clipper, flight 114, she says. She was accompanied by her husband, a medical doctor. Her exploration was largely in getting to know Schweitzer and his wife, and how they treated their patients. The effects on her of anti-malaria pills. We hear the sounds of very different animals in the night than travelers in the American West would have heard. There is a visit to a leper colony. The living conditions for her in Africa were primitive, but better than most American pioneers could have dreamed of. The duration of Ethyle's trip to Africa was very short compared to the many months folks spent on the trails West. But her days were full, and still she kept a journal.

I think what I learned from these women, the American pioneers of the nineteenth century and the mid-twentieth century adventurer Ethyle Town is that if you want to write, you will write. No excuses. Just do it, as they say. You are not too tired to write. You are not too busy or frazzled. You can do it.

And the stories! You will save the stories. The grand life of travel is no more important than yours. Never forget that.

CHAPTER TWENTY-TWO

THERE ARE SOME STORIES that will stay with me forever. The people, the circumstances, haunt me still, after so many years.

One of the more challenging and compelling stories I wrote for the *Chicago Tribune* involved interviewing women who gave birth while incarcerated. I wrote this story more than twenty-five years ago. Maybe conditions are better for pregnant women in jail today, but it was fairly recently that I read that a woman was forced to give birth on the floor of her cell, her hands shackled. So maybe conditions are not better.

It was not an easy story to report. For one thing, officials at the Cook County Jail in Chicago, where I did my interviews, were reluctant to talk to me. The situation was complicated by politics as a recent election was causing a change in personnel. But eventually I was able to talk to several women. My interest was never in the politics. I very quickly realized that I didn't care too much about the causes of the situation being so harsh – overcrowding, financial issues that caused the women to be unable to make bail, etc. – because it was so gut-wrenching to hear their stories. It was very hard to be objective. I could only think of the negative effects on the mothers and their babies. That was all I could focus on.

First the mothers. They had committed crimes ranging from

petty larceny to murder. But the ones I interviewed were not hardened criminals. Even one I met who had murdered her abusive partner in what she felt was her only recourse to protect herself and her children. She was a confused, trapped, terrified victim. Many of the women had other children at home. The women I interviewed were all pregnant when they committed their crimes.

Most said they were under the impression that they were going to be able to keep their babies with them after they were born. In truth, the babies were removed one or two days after birth. If there were family members who could take care of them, at least the mother knew where the baby was. If not, the child went into foster care. Visitations were often as few as once a month. The women could communicate with their families through a glass window. No touching between mother and child was allowed. Some women were so heartbroken they didn't even want the visits. It was too painful.

And the babies suffered even more, though they weren't aware of it. Deprived of the early bonding that is so important between mother and child, many of these children would grow up to have developmental and other issues that would affect their chances of success in school and later in life.

The women, who may not have had much insight into their lives when they committed their crimes, did seem to have learned a lot while in jail. One said to me "I can change, but I can't make up this time. It's not me who has the pressure; it's my children." Of course. It's a horrible story, and another example of how women often pay a terrible price for being trapped in situations where they have no good options. Just because they are women.

Around the same time, I tackled two stories on immigrant families in Chicago. Written two years apart, they both focused on the hardships of adjusting to life in a new culture. And in particular, since these stories, like the prison story, were written for the woman's section of the *Chicago Tribune*, my focus was on the burden of adjustment that fell on the wives and mothers of the families.

I interviewed several families. They came from places that ranged from Poland to Viet Nam to Korea. The mothers struggled with language issues, with helping their children to adjust to new schools, with comforting husbands who frequently couldn't find jobs that equaled in prestige the ones they'd had in their former lives. Sometimes the husbands had emigrated a year or two ahead of their wives. Then, while waiting for their wife's papers to be in order for the trip, they may have found another woman, maybe even had another child. Typically they wouldn't be knowledgeable about how to stop the immigration process for the wife, so she would arrive and move in but the marriage was really over. Sometimes there was violence. Some women in this situation would want to return to their home countries but they'd have sold everything and would not even be able to find an apartment easily. They'd burned their bridges and were stuck.

Another common theme was that even in families where the original marriage remained intact, there was often strife because the woman was able to find better work than her husband could. Or she learned the new language more easily. Coming from cultures where the man felt he was superior – he was the authority figure and believed he needed to be the major breadwinner in order to remain superior – this was often difficult for both husband and wife to accept. The wife was left to smooth things over, make concessions so her husband did not feel threatened.

These stories are based on interviews I did many years ago. Imagine the stress today, now that they find themselves in a country that seems openly hostile to immigrants, even those who have followed all the rules and are in the U.S. legally.

In every family I interviewed it was the woman who bore the burden and the woman who held the family together if that was possible. Their stories were all different in detail but they shared a common thread: strength. No less than the strength of the early pioneers, of the Crypto-Jews, of the women who sewed their stories into their tablecloths in their own secret Nu Shu script. It was their determination to tell their stories that kept them strong. I saw it in their faces, in the way they moved their hands. They wanted to be heard. That is what gave me the strength to help them tell their stories. And that is why I made the extra effort to really listen, to absorb and try to understand the essence of lives that were so different from mine. Permanently moving to a different country. Living part or all of a life in prison. I had no experience; I had to really listen.

It's true that I gravitate toward women's stories. I have written about men also. I told you about Clayton Moore and John Mahoney and O.J. Simpson. There were many others too, some good some bad. But there is something terribly compelling about the lives of the women I met. Maybe it was best described by whoever said of Ginger Rogers that she did the same thing as Fred Astaire, and just as well, but she did it backwards and in high heels. The obstacles are often greater for women just because they are women.

Eva Kor, for instance, who started a Holocaust museum in Terre Haute, Indiana. What were her credentials for doing such a thing? No particular training. Just lucky? Oh, that's right, she was a Mengele twin. She and her twin sister, Miriam, were experimented on at Auschwitz, by the evil Dr. Mengele, with the intention of killing them both when the experiment was completed. They both survived because the camp was liberated before the experiment ended. Or Rosa Parks. She sat down at the front of the bus and refused to move. *She* did that. Not a man. Or popular mystery writer, P.D. James, who wrote her first novel while riding to work on the London Tube to a job she needed to support her family because her husband was shell-shocked (now we call it PTSD) as a result of service in WWII. Yes, I talked to these women. And how about the millions of women over the centuries that I didn't speak with? For whom nobody has recorded a story. Whose accomplishments were monumental, nonetheless.

We must tell our stories. And help others to do so, too, if we are able.

CHAPTER TWENTY-THREE

WHAT WAS THE RESULT of all this writing? Where did it all go?

Honestly, not a word, not a moment, was wasted. I can't tell whether I learned more about other people or more about myself, but it really doesn't matter. In the end, I wrote more than five hundred articles for various publications, about four hundred of them for the *Chicago Tribune*. I wrote a novel based on the stories written by the Nu Shu ladies. I wrote a workbook about how to write and organize your memories so at the very least you will have recorded your stories for your family. Finally, I found a way to tell my grandmother's story of how she learned to read in a time and place where girls were not allowed to attend school – a children's book was the answer to that one. And I did a lot of teaching, too. I taught elementary school and I taught college classes about writing and literature. I started a novel about Conversos and Crypto-Jews and someday it might be finished. I started a few other novels that will most likely never be finished.

And I met people. People with stories. People who trusted me with their stories. I hope I did right by them. And I wrote some of my own stories. I hope I did right by them too. I think I did.

And where is the little girl who tried to write a mystery at age eight, whose fourth-grade teacher envisioned her as a writer, whose essay came in second place when she was twelve? She's still there, maybe a bit more sure of herself, but still trying to get the story right, whether it's hers or someone else's.

But most of all, meeting people and listening to stories and writing stories did something else for me. It made me think. About all the varieties of life. All the ways folks take the circumstances of their being on this planet and deal with them. Or don't. Those who tell their stories are thinking about their lives. They're looking for patterns, for reasons. They're trying to make it work.

Those who don't tell their stories, who hide from them, who run from them, well, I don't know what to say about that. I hope they will stop and look at themselves. And listen to themselves. Make some notes. Tell a story they remember from childhood. Tell another one. Remember one they thought they'd forgotten and tell that one, too. It is because I feel so strongly about the benefits of such an exercise that I decided to add an afterword to this book. It's meant to help you get started. I hope you will.

Read on.

AFTERWORD

SO HERE'S A CONFESSION. You know the part in Chapter Twelve where I talk about my grandmother? How she told us about the woman who fell out of a moving car? How she called everything a machine? It's not exactly true.

Oh, it all happened. But not with one grandmother. It's a compilation of facts about both my grandmothers. And I don't remember either of them reading the street signs but my father did, on the two occasions late in his life when he let me drive him somewhere for some reason I can't remember. It must have been monumentally important. Or it would never have happened. He, who always drove a stick shift car, gave me some credit for driving one too. But when he sat down in the passenger seat and saw that my car had five gears, not three, he put his hands up to his cheeks and said in amazement, "How do you like that?" And he is the one who read the signs as we passed them in a not so subtle attempt to keep me on the straight and narrow.

Is that kosher? Can you mix up who said what in a memoir? Is it accurate? Well, here's the thing about memory: try as you might you'll never get everything exactly as it happened anyway. I'm not suggesting that you lie. And certainly not that you defame or embarrass anyone. But like it or not – and whether you know it or not – you will probably get some of the details wrong. Especially when you're looking way back in time. Our memories are not infallible. Not even close.

Have I hurt anyone by combining elements of both grandmothers and my father into one story? I don't think so. Maybe you have a different opinion. That's okay. But this is my memoir. It's my story and I'm allowed to tell it however I want.

A further confession. When I first started writing that little bit about my grandmother in the car I really did think it was all one person. (It all happened more than sixty years ago – give me a break.) But as I continued to write, it became clear what I was unconsciously doing. I liked the way it worked so I kept it that way. Sue me!

But this illustrates a bonus to writing down what you remember about your own story. The more you write, the more you'll remember. And it will become clearer. That's a promise.

When I moved to New Mexico I began giving writing workshops: travel writing, article writing, how to deal with writer's block. But what became the most popular was my workshop on memoir writing. I had already been teaching writing, along with literature and humanities courses as an adjunct instructor at Oakton Community College in Illinois, something I did along with my freelance writing, for twenty years. When I designed the memoir writing workshop in New Mexico I wrote a workbook to go along with the class. That helped me crystalize my ideas about how to collect stories and how to tell them. I think, in many ways, the story about the story can be just as interesting as the story itself – whether you are talking about your own life, or about how you learned something of another person's life.

Here is another confession. This book was written in two parts. With a ten-year break between the sections. The original manuscript, comprising a little less than half the finished book, was discovered following a computer melt-down. I lost part of another manuscript I was working on, and in attempting to find it I happened upon another book, this one, halfway finished. It's not just that I had forgotten about it, which I had, it's also that even when I read through it and knew it had to have been written by me, I still couldn't remember the actual act of writing it.

Where was I when I did it? My office was in a different part of the house in those days. I tried to picture myself at the desk that used to be in that office, writing away at this book, but no vision would come to mind. Why did I start writing it? And, more to the point, why did I stop? Was there a story I didn't want to tell? Was I blocked because of events going on in my life at that time? Or did I just lose the momentum, put it aside for a while to work on other things, and forget all about it? That hardly seems possible, but I did forget, and I'm afraid I don't know why.

Even stranger than all this is the fact that for about a year before finding the unfinished manuscript, I'd been playing around in my mind with an idea for a book that would be a memoir about writing and would incorporate stories of the work I'd done. In other words, I was planning how to write a book that was already half written. What we don't know about how our minds work is surely one of the biggest mysteries of life.

When I read through the manuscript as it existed at the time I found it, I removed some stories. Sorry. I just didn't think they were appropriate. Maybe I stopped writing because I was conflicted about including those stories. Too revealing? Not really honest? Unfair to someone? Maybe I needed ten years more of maturity to make the right decision about them. But then I have to ask the old question again: What happens to the stories we don't tell? The great writing teacher, Natalie Goldberg, who has developed the method of free writing practice to a fine art, says in *Let the Whole Thundering World Come Home*, "The things we avoid have energy." Was I avoiding something so powerful that it made me stop writing?

I've read a lot of memoirs. I've taught countless workshops in memoir writing. I have to tell you there are some stories that don't need to see the light of day in print. Still, I believe that those are decisions the author has the right to make for herself. And a serious consideration in making the decision would be whether or not she intends to publish her story or just keep it for herself or her family. I never told a student to omit something. Often they asked my opinion. I didn't give one. I told them it was their story; that they should write what they want to write, tell what they want to tell. Sometimes, though, I suggested they consult a lawyer if they were planning to publish.

It is eternally true that the more you write, the more you'll remember. (That, by the way, is one of the great benefits of writing down your stories.) I remember the way people looked when I interviewed them, for instance, and how I interpreted their mannerisms then, compared to how some of it seems to me now. I remember how their voices sounded when they spoke. That can reveal a lot about how a person feels, once you have some practice in listening.

The same has happened regarding some of the stories I told here of my childhood. The one about my mother taking driving lessons behind my father's back, for instance. That event happened more than sixty years ago. Yet I can see it vividly still. Certainly it made a strong impression on me. And it's pretty obvious why it did so. It no doubt colored my view of women in the world, and marriage, and who knows what else. I know as a teenager living at home I didn't fight my father's view that women shouldn't drive. I just didn't drive a car until I was twenty. I know I wouldn't be so passive about it today.

I've actually written that story about my mother a few times in my life, generally for one writing workshop or another. I always view it slightly differently. In the past I saw my parents as comic characters. "Wasn't that just like them?" I would think with a chuckle. My mother's behavior was out of character as far as taking the lessons in secret, but not in how she fell apart when challenged by my father. His behavior was right in character. Now I see it as a more serious event. I wonder if it changed the dynamic of their marriage forever. Or was it just one more restriction she agreed to accept? And I wonder if he ever felt guilty about what he did. As I've said before, he was not a hurtful man.

There is a huge bonus in revisiting old memories and, especially, rethinking them. I've heard many discussions about how an artist knows when her painting is finished. Working on this book has made me realize it's the same for writing. I see things more deeply now than I did when I wrote the first part of the manuscript. Should I wait ten years after finishing the rest, just in case? No, I won't. That is not feasible given the life expectancy of the author, or at least of the author's brain. But what a gift it has been to reread the old part of the story and tell the rest of it now.

DECIDING WHERE TO START is what holds most people back from beginning to tell their story. The answer to this question is fairly simple. But first you have to answer another question: What kind of story do you want to tell? If you want to write your autobiography, or a biography of someone else, you start at the beginning. Either of these types of story is a recounting of a person's life and it should be presented in chronological order.

But a memoir is something quite different. This book, for instance, is a memoir. It only tells about one aspect of my life – my experiences as a writer, with a little bit about my childhood and my teaching life where it seemed appropriate – and it's not presented in chronological order. That affords me the leeway to present episodes in whatever order I feel will have the most impact. Or seems to make the most sense. An additional advantage to choosing to tell your story as a memoir is that you can write individual vignettes and worry about the order later. And it won't be much of a worry because as you write your memories down, a pattern will emerge.

An elderly gentleman in one of my workshops told me that he had written quite a number of stories when it occurred to him that almost every story had a dog in it. Over the course of seventy-plus years of life he had had many canine companions. It came to him in a jolt of recognition that he should organize his memoir around the different dogs in his life. Another workshop participant was toying with the idea of naming her memoir "Bathrooms I Have Known." She'd been writing about all the various homes she'd lived in and countries she'd visited and, suddenly, there it was. Neither of them would have thought of their title or method of organization before they started writing. So go ahead and tell the stories and you can have confidence that a pattern will emerge.

Which brings us to the next point of business: How to remember the stories. Of course, you remember many. But how to elicit more? The simple truth is, the more you write, the more you will remember. If you are even thinking of writing a memoir, you already have something you want to tell. So tell it. Write it down quickly. Don't worry about punctuation or spelling. Or structure, for that matter. Just get it out. (There will be time to correct mistakes later.) In the course of writing this story, other memories will pop into your head. When I write I keep a pad of paper next to my computer so I can quickly jot down anything that comes to me and turn right back to the story I'm working on. That way I have ideas in the pipeline that may or may not prove useful somewhere else.

If you can't get started, if nothing is coming to you some morning, open an old picture album, or a book or newspaper, or look out the window. Choose a random word in the dictionary and try to start a sentence with it. Something will make you think of something else and then you'll be off and running. Start writing. And remember: if it turns out that this jogs a memory that is unpleasant and you don't want to deal with it, then don't. Go through the process again and write something else. Maybe this is not the right time to remember this story. It's your decision.

Just a few more words about memory. What, exactly is it? I checked a few dictionaries and found a variety of takes on the subject. One defines it as the mental faculty of retaining and recalling past experiences. Another simply says it is all that a person can remember. Still another calls it the fact of being remembered.

Whatever it is, it's elusive. For instance, how do we know we are remembering an event correctly? Is it a memory if it is inaccurate? Actually, a memory is the truth as you remember it. Have you ever read an eyewitness account of an event you yourself also witnessed? Was the account exactly the same as you remember it? Probably not. We all remember selectively and our memories are colored by our life experiences. That's why several people can testify at a trial, all swear to tell the truth and mean it, and all have slightly different stories to tell.

Your memory is the truth as you remember it. And the memoir you write is your telling of that truth as you remember it. Or as you want to remember it. Or as you feel it's necessary to remember it in order to tell a good story. This doesn't mean you lie about essential facts. That would take it into the realm of fiction. But it is your story, even if your mother, father, brother or sister remember it in a different way. It's possible that as you proceed in collecting the stories of your life, you will talk to people about certain events in order to get more information. This is fine. But please remember that just because someone's version of a story differs from yours it doesn't mean you are wrong. It doesn't mean the other person is wrong, either. Lots of things contribute to how and what we remember: other events in our lives, stresses or emotional difficulties, even our birth order can color how we see a family story.

Please write your story. If only for yourself. Memories will reappear. Secrets will unfold. You will see old stories in a new light; you will rescue the stories that haven't been told. As the memories come back to you, remember to listen to them. What are they telling you now? How is it different from what you thought at the time the events were happening? You will be richly rewarded for the effort. That's a promise.

ACKNOWLEDGEMENTS

As always, I must thank the women who invented and used the Nu Shu writing system to record and save their stories, as well as to open a window on their personal lives for historical purposes. Even though I was already a writer when I encountered their work, they have consistently inspired me to examine and tell my own story. To put it in writing and to encourage others to do the same. Thanks, as always, to Su Chien-ling, who guided me in listening to and understanding the stories. And I want to thank author Jacqueline Tobin who encouraged me, for many years, to turn the Nu Shu stories into a book. And thank you to the many editors at the *Chicago Tribune* who gave me the opportunity to hone my craft and to meet so many engaging, stimulating, and inspiring people.

Thanks, too, to Dr. Stanley Hordes, who helped me learn about the Converso/Crypto-Jewish community in New Mexico and taught me the interviewing techniques I would need to further my research. Also, thanks to the women pioneers who found a way to write after the busiest of days anyone can imagine, and to Judy McNett, who helped me sort out the life of twentieth century pioneer, Ethyle Town.

I would like to express my appreciation to the people who supported me in the writing of this book by reading, listening, or commenting: Harry Guffee, Mary Carter, Joan Jander, Gwenellen Janov, Beverly Ledbetter, Daisy Kates and, for being a stable influence in the background, Dorothy Hudson. Special thanks to Gary Priester for much needed and appreciated technical support and for designing this book. Thank you, Jay Harrison, for publishing my writing, some of which became part of this book, at Boomspeak.com. And thank you, David Steinberg, for editing and helping me organize my manuscript into a sensible whole. Thanks, always, to the late Francis Roe, who assured me I could do it. My deepest gratitude to my brothers and sisters, to whom this book is dedicated, for reading the manuscript and helping me gain perspective on the past. And to Dan, Molly, Amy, Joseph, Marc, Christina, Benny, Madeleine, Miya, Rose, Oscar, and Miles, who are my life and my loves.

STUDY GUIDE FOR READERS AND WRITERS

This book contains two study guides. The Readers Study Guide is meant to be used by book clubs or other discussion groups, or in classrooms or writing workshops.

The Writers Guide is designed to help those who wish to collect their own memories and write a memoir or autobiography for themselves, their family, or to publish. It contains suggestions for retrieving memories and getting them down on paper.

I do hope that these materials will enhance the experience of reading this book.

READERS STUDY GUIDE

The following questions are presented as a guide to discussion in a book club or workshop setting, or for personal introspection.

1. Why does Libman feel such an affinity for the users of Nu Shu?

2. How did the Conversos and pioneer women inspire her?

3. How do the stories from Libman's own life relate to the stories of the people she has written about? What has she learned from both sets of stories?

4. What does Libman say about the stories we don't tell? Does she think they are important?

5. What has Libman learned about the importance of listening?

6. What do you think she has learned from her failed writings? Why do you think she included those stories in this memoir?

7. Do you see a pattern in the lives of the women who inspired Libman? If so, what is it?

8. What do you think about the men she has referenced or whose lives she has chosen to describe?

9. Libman selected fewer men to include in this book than women. Why do you think this might be?

10. In some ways it seems as though this could be two books: one, the story of the author's life as a writer; the other, background on the people she met and wrote about. Do you think this book could be divided into two separate books? Why or why not?

WRITERS STUDY GUIDE

"The unexamined life is not worth living."

—Socrates

Socrates' words may be a bit of an exaggeration, but I do believe that the examined life is richer than one that is lived in a foggy haze of jumping from one thing to another without stopping to look at the full picture. Many of us do that for years before we find the time or the inclination to slow down and look back and try to see what caused what, why we did what we did, and think about what we want to do now.

If this is that time for you, I hope some of my suggested topics listed below will get you started and that you'll find the process enjoyable. Dive in and pick a topic from anywhere on the list. Set yourself a certain amount of time to write. No editing or correcting grammar or spelling. Just write for the allotted time. Ten minutes is good for a starter. Then reread what you wrote and put it aside. The next day pick another topic. Most of them can be repeated many times. You'll probably want to expand to longer writing times as you get more comfortable. There are no rules about how long you write or what time of day you do it. Whatever works for you is just right. Don't try to edit anything you've written for at least two or three days. Waiting longer is even better. But do try to write something every day. Or at least five days a week. The more you write, the more you'll remember. And that will make you want to keep the pen moving or the keyboard humming.

Here are some topics to get you started. You'll probably think of more as you get into the rhythm of examining and writing about your life.

A day at school

A religious experience

Where and how you learned to drive

A smell you remember

A favorite trip you took as a child

Your relationship with your parents

A hospital you spent some time in

Your grandmother's house

Your best friend

Your wedding

Your children

Your grandchildren

Your nickname

A family story you remember differently than others do

Something that puzzled you when you were a child

A divorce

Memories of music

A terrible fight or disagreement with someone

An accident

Your career or job

Your greatest belief

Humorous events

The most unusual person you've known

Your most important relative

Your funniest relative

Someone who has betrayed you

Your favorite book or movie

The most daring thing you've done

Something that scares you

Something your intuition has told you

A favorite memory concerning sports

A death that you've never gotten over

A beautiful place

This is only the beginning. The more you write, the more you'll think of writing. Go for it!

ABOUT THE AUTHOR

Norma Libman is a journalist and educator. She is the author of more than 500 articles published in newspapers nationwide, and has written an award-winning novel, *Lonely River Village*, based on her ground-breaking research on Nu Shu, the secret Chinese women's writing system. Libman has also written a children's book, *Hannah's Day at School*. She lives, writes, and teaches in New Mexico.

Visit her website: www.NormaLibman.com

38655975R00097

Made in the USA
Middletown, DE
12 March 2019